THE CHILD PROTECTION INVESTIGATOR'S COMPANION

revised second edition

Kevin Smith

With contributions by Alan Beckley on the Human Rights Act 1998

The Child Protection Investigator's Companion

First edition 1994
Police Review Publishing Co

Second edition 1999
Reprinted 2000
The New Police Bookshop

Revised second edition August 2001

ISBN: 1 903639 04 2

Published by
The New Police Bookshop
(Benson Publications) Surrey

Printed and bound in Great Britain by
Antony Rowe Ltd, Chippenham, Wiltshire

Orders and customer services
Brookland Mailing Services, Unit 4, Parkway Trading Estate
St Werburghs Road, St Werburghs, Bristol BS2 9PG
Tel 0117 9555 215 Fax 0117 9541 485
Email npb@brookland-mailing.co.uk

Enquiries may be directed to:
NPB Promotion
PO Box 2, Much Wenlock TF13 6WL
Email NPBpromotion@aol.com

www.newpolicebookshop.co.uk

The author

Kevin Smith worked for some years on a Child Protection Team in South London up until 1995. During this time he investigated a number of instance of child abuse and was involved in the joint training of police officers and social workers.

Since leaving child protection, he has worked in more general investigative training.

Kevin Smith has a first class honours degree in psychology, a masters degree in education and a PhD in social psychology.

Contributor on human rights

Alan Beckley has served for 29 years in the police service, and is a serving police officer in West Mercia Constabulary with the rank of Chief Inspector.

Since 1998, he has been a part time member of the ACPO committee on human rights and policing.

Alan Beckley has had many articles on policing and legal subjects published, has written several books on operational policing and human rights and is the Managing Editor of two police journals, *Police Research & Management* and *Policing, Ethics and Human Rights.*

Preface to the first edition

This book is for the broad range of practitioners involved in the initial investigation of child protection cases. *The Child Protection Investigator's Companion* is intended to provide investigators from any agency involved in child protection work with readily accessible information in respect of their responsibilities, powers and duties during the initial phase of a child protection inquiry.

It also provides a great deal of guidance in respect of the criminal offences that may be encountered during the course of such investigation and is up to date as far as the Criminal Justice and Public Order Act 1994, although the reader will need to take account of the rolling introduction of the various parts of this Act.

This book may, therefore, be read as an introduction to initial child protection investigations and then kept as a source book by practitioners for easy reference when the need arises during such inquiries.

Kevin Smith, 1994

Preface to the second edition

Since the publication of the first edition to *The Child Protection Investigator's Companion*, a great deal has changed in respect of the legislation concerned with child protection, notably in terms of sexual offences and sex offenders. This new edition takes account of these changes.

Kevin Smith, March 1999

Preface to the revised second edition

Since the publication of the second edition, there have been major developments relating to human rights in the enactments of the Human Rights Act 1998 (HRA). Police officers now have a duty to positively uphold and protect the human rights of citizens. Specifically, officers have a duty to take measures to protect life, including a duty to put in place effective criminal law provisions to deter the commission of offences against the person backed up by law enforcement machinery for the prevention, suppression and sanctioning of breaches for such provisions. Consequently, there is a greater emphasis on the prevention and protection role and responsibility of police officers; this is especially so in relation to child victims. Child Protection has therefore assumed an even higher importance in the police response to prevent and detect crime. This revised edition takes account of the changes and is also updated in respect of the Youth Justice and Criminal Evidence Act 1999, the Criminal Justice and Court Services Act 2000 and the Sexual Offences (Amendment) Act 2000.

Kevin Smith, August 2001

Table of contents

Chapter 5: Cruelty and neglect

Chapter 6: Offences relating to pregnancy

Chapter 7: Abduction

PART THREE: POLICE POWERS

Chapter 8: Powers of arrest

Chapter 9: Powers to search

Chapter 10: Human Rights

PART FOUR: EVIDENCE

Chapter 11
Interviews and medical examinations - consent of victims

Chapter 12
Taking samples from suspects

Chapter 13
Video interviewing child witnesses

Chapter 14
Preparing child witnesses to give evidence

Chapter 15

PART ONE

PROTECTION ORDERS AND CARE

1. Police protection
2. Protection orders

This part of the book has been set out according to the speed with which it might be deemed necessary to take action in child protection matters. Any decision made in this respect should always be based upon the safety and welfare of the child.

CHAPTER 1

POLICE PROTECTION

1.1. The role of police in child protection

'Police involvement in cases of child abuse stems from their primary responsibilities to protect the community and to bring offenders to justice. Their overriding consideration is the welfare of the child.'

(Paragraph 4.11 of 'Working Together Under The Children Act 1989')

There is also the positive duty on police officers to uphold and protect the rights of individuals under the Human Rights Act 1998.

1.2. Removal and accommodation of children by police in cases of emergency

Section 46 Children Act 1989

Ss (1)

If a constable has reasonable cause to believe that a child would otherwise be likely to suffer **'significant harm'**, she or he may:

a. remove the child to suitable accommodation and keep her or him there; or

b. take such steps as are reasonable to ensure that the child's removal from any hospital, or other place, in which she or he is then being accommodated, is prevented.

Ss (2)

For the purposes of this Act a child - with respect to whom a constable has exercised her or his powers under this Section - is referred to as having being taken into **'police protection'**.

Ss (3)

As soon as is reasonably practicable, after taking a child into police protection, the constable concerned shall:

(a) inform the local authority, within whose area the child was found, of the steps that have been and are proposed to be taken with respect to the child under this Section, and the reasons for taking them;

(b) give details to the authority within whose area the child is ordinarily resident - the **'appropriate authority'** (see 2.1) - of the place at which the child is being accommodated;

(c) inform the child (if she or he appears capable of understanding) -
   i. of the steps that have been taken with respect to her or him under this Section, and of the reasons for taking them, and
   ii. of the further steps that may be taken with respect to her or him under this Section;

(d) take such steps as are reasonably practicable to discover the wishes and feelings of the child;

(e) ensure that the case is inquired into by an **'officer designated'** for the purposes of this Section by the chief officer of the Police Area concerned; and

(f) in cases in which the child was taken into police protection by being removed to accommodation which is not provided -
   i. by or on behalf of a local authority, or
   ii. as a refuge in compliance with the requirements of Section 51,

   ensure that she or he is moved to accommodation which is so provided.

Ss (4)

As soon as is reasonably practicable after taking a child into police protection, the constable concerned shall take such steps as are reasonably practicable to inform:

(a) the child's parents;

(b) every person who is not a parent of hers or his but who has **'parental responsibility'** for her or him; and

(c) any other person with whom the child was living immediately before being taken into police protection;

of the steps that the constable has taken under this Section with respect to the child, the reasons for taking them, and the further steps that may be taken with respect to her or him under this Section.

Ss (5)

On completing any inquiry under Sub-section (3)(e) above, the officer conducting it shall release the child from police protection unless she or he considers that there is still reasonable cause to believe that the child would be likely to suffer significant harm if released.

Ss (6)

No child may be kept in police protection for more than 72 hours.

Ss (7)

While a child is being kept in police protection, the designated officer may apply on behalf of the appropriate authority (see 2.1) for an emergency protection order (see 2.2) to be made under Section 44 with respect to the child.

Ss (8)

An application may be made under Sub-section (7) irrespective of whether the authority knows of it or agrees to its being made.

Ss (9)

While a child is being kept in police protection:

(a) neither the constable concerned nor the designated officer shall have parental responsibility for her or him; but

(b) the designated officer shall do what is reasonable in all the circumstances of the case for the purpose of safeguarding or promoting the child's welfare (having regard in particular to the length of the period during which the child will be so protected).

Ss (10)

When a child has been taken into police protection, the designated officer shall allow:

(a) the child's parents;

(b) any person who is not a parent of the child but who has parental responsibility for her or him;

(c) any person with whom the child was living immediately before she or he was taken into police protection;

(d) any person in whose favour a contact order is in force with respect to the child;

(e) any person who is allowed to have contact with the child by virtue of an order under Section 34 (parental contact etc with children in care); and

(f) any person acting on behalf of any of those persons;

to have such contact (if any) with the child as, in the opinion of the designated officer, is both reasonable and in the child's best interests.

Ss (11)

When a child, who has been taken into police protection, is in accommodation provided by or on behalf of the appropriate authority, Sub-section (10) shall have effect as if referring to the authority rather than to the designated officer.

Notes

This power to remove and accommodate children should be exercised sparingly by police officers. It is an emergency power that should only be used if it is not possible to leave a child in any given situation for the few hours it will take to apply to a court (or, outside court hours, to a Justice of the Peace) without putting or leaving them at risk of significant harm.

'Significant harm' is defined by Section 31(9) and (10) of this Act - as set out in Application for Care Orders and Supervision Orders (see 2.4b).

'Parental responsibility' within the terms of the Children Act 1989 means the child's:

i. natural mother;
ii. natural father if the child's parents were married at the time of the child's birth;
iii. natural father if a **'parental responsibility agreement'** has been drawn up in the form prescribed by the Lord Chancellor; and
iv. any person having parental responsibility by virtue of some form of court order;

(Sections 2 and 4 Children Act 1989 etc).

Note that the use of police protection does NOT give police officers parental rights. This is particularly notable in terms of consent to medical examinations (see 11.1 (Notes)).

'Designated officer' refers to police officers nominated specifically to perform this function by the Chief Officer of Police for any given force. While working in the child protection field it may be worth your while finding out which police officers in the area in which you are working have been so designated.

Human Rights implications: Police officers should bear in mind the effects of the Human Rights Act 1998 on decisions they make relating to Child Protection. Police officers now have a duty to positively uphold and protect the human rights of citizens, especially children as they are a vulnerable section of society. When deciding to use police powers relating to Protection Orders and Care, ECHR Article 8 (Right to Respect for Private and Family Life) should be carefully considered before taking action. For further details, see Chapter 10.

For an overview of this Section see Fig 1 overleaf.

FIG 1: POLICE PROTECTION

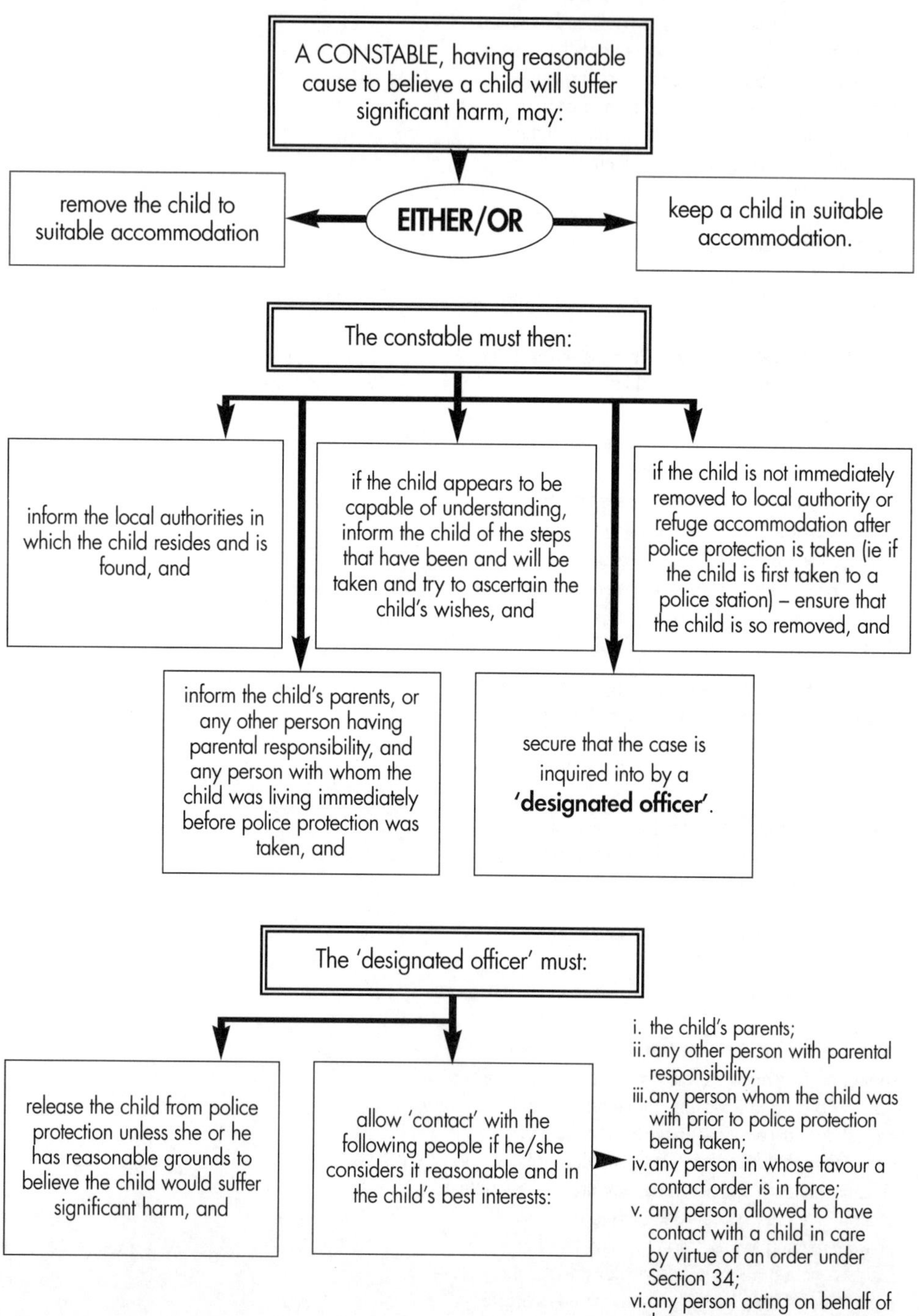

CHAPTER 2

PROTECTION ORDERS

Applications - who may apply?

Any person (including police officers) may apply for an emergency protection order. Only the local authority or an authorised person (the NSPCC) may apply for the other orders (with the exception of residence or contact orders) set out below.

It seems likely that the majority of applications for the orders that follow will be made by local authority social workers. It may, therefore, be useful to consider the duty local authorities have with regard to investigating child protection matters before considering these orders in a little more detail.

2.1. The duty of local authorities to investigate

Section 47 Children Act 1989 as amended by the Health Authorities Act 1995

Ss (1)

When a local authority:

(a) is informed that a child, who lives or is found in its area -
  i. is the subject of an emergency protection order, or
  ii. is in police protection; or

(b) has reasonable cause to suspect that a child, who lives or is found in its area, is suffering or is likely to suffer significant harm;

the authority shall make, or cause to be made, such inquiries as it considers necessary to enable it to decide whether it should take any action to safeguard or promote the child's welfare.

Ss (2)

When a local authority has obtained an emergency protection order (see 2.2) with respect to a child, it shall make, or cause to be made, such inquiries as it considers necessary to enable it to decide whether it should take any action to safeguard or promote the child's welfare.

Ss (3)

The inquiries shall, in particular, be directed towards establishing whether:

(a) the authority should make any application to the court, or exercise any other of its powers under this Act, with respect to the child;

(b) in the case of a child -
  i. with respect to whom an emergency protection order has been made, and
  ii. who is not in accommodation provided by or on behalf of the authority;

  it would be in the child's best interests (while an emergency protection order remains in force) for her or him to be in such accommodation; and

(c) in the case of a child who has been taken into police protection, it would be in the child's best interests for the authority to ask for an application to be made to obtain an emergency protection order.

Ss (4)

When inquiries are being made under Sub-section (1) with respect to a child, the local authority concerned shall (with a view to enabling it to determining what action, if any, to take with respect to her or him) take such steps as are reasonably practicable:

(a) to obtain access to her or him;

(b) to ensure that access to her or him is obtained, on its behalf, by a person authorised by the authority, for the purpose;

unless it is satisfied that it already has sufficient information with respect to her or him.

Ss (5)

When, as a result of any such inquiries, it appears to the authority that there are matters connected to the child's education which should be investigated, it shall consult the relevant local education authority.

Ss (6)

When, in the course of inquiries made under this Section, any officer of the local authority concerned or any person authorised by the authority to Act on its behalf in connection with those inquiries:

(a) is refused access to the child concerned; or

(b) is denied information as to her or his whereabouts,

the authority shall apply for –

i. an emergency protection order,
ii. a child assessment order,
iii. a care order, or
iv. a supervision order,

with respect to the child, unless it is satisfied her or his welfare can be satisfactorily safeguarded without so doing.

Ss (7)

If, on the conclusion of any inquiries or review made under this Section, the authority decides not to apply for an emergency protection order, a child assessment order, a care order or a supervision order it shall:

(a) consider whether it would be appropriate to review the case at a later date; and

(b) if it so decides, determine the date on which that review will begin.

Ss (8)

When, as a result of complying with this Section, a local authority concludes that it should take action to safeguard or promote the child's welfare, it shall take action (so far as it is both within its power and is reasonably practicable to undertake).

Ss (9)

When a local authority is conducting inquiries under this Section, it shall be the duty of any **'person'** mentioned in Sub-section (11) to assist with those inquiries (in particular by providing relevant information and advice) if called upon by the authority to do so.

Ss (10)

Sub-section (9) does not oblige any person to assist a local authority if to do so would be unreasonable in all the circumstances of the case.

Ss (11)

The **'persons'** are:

(a) any local authority;

(b) any local education authority;

(c) any local housing authority;

(d) any Health Authority, Special Health Authority or National Health Service Trust; and

(e) any person authorised by the Secretary of State for the purposes of this Section.

Ss (12)

When a local authority is making inquiries under this Section with respect to a child who appears to it to be ordinarily resident within the area of another local authority, it shall consult that other local authority, who may undertake the necessary inquiries in its place.

Note

Two important principles should be borne in mind while investigations are conducted under this Section:

1. That when a court determines any question with respect either to the upbringing of a child or the administration of a child's property, the child's welfare shall be of paramount consideration.

2. That the concept of a partnership with parents and other family members, with a view to supporting the child within the family whenever possible, is a concept implicit to the Children Act (and explicit in Paragraph 5.4 'Working Together under the Children Act 1989').

2.2. Emergency protection orders

Section 44 Children Act 1989

For an overview of this Section see Fig 2 overleaf.

Ss (1)

When any person - **'the applicant'** - applies to the court for an order to be made under this Section with respect to a child, the court may make the order if, and only if, it is satisfied that:

(a) there is reasonable cause to believe that the child is likely to suffer **'significant harm'** if -
  i. she or he is not removed to accommodation provided by or on behalf of the applicant,
  ii. she or he does not remain in the place in which she or he is then being accommodated;

(b) in the case of an application made by a local authority -
  i. inquiries are being made with respect to the child under Section 47 (1)(b) - making inquiries as a result of having cause to suspect a child in its area is suffering or likely to suffer significant harm, and
  ii. those inquiries are being frustrated by access to the child being unreasonably refused to a **'person authorised to seek access'** and that the applicant has reasonable cause to believe that access to the child is required as a matter of urgency; or

(c) in the case of an application made by an **'authorised person'** -
  i. the applicant has reasonable cause to suspect that a child is suffering, or is likely to suffer, significant harm,
  ii. the applicant is making inquiries with respect to the child's welfare, and
  iii. those inquiries are being frustrated by access to the child being unreasonably refused to a person authorised to seek access and the applicant has reasonable cause to believe that access to the child is required as a matter of urgency.

Ss (2)

In this Section:

(a) **'authorised person'** means a person who is an authorised person for the purposes of Section 31 as outlined in S31(9) (which does not include the police - see applications for care and supervision orders, 2.4b); and

(b) **'person authorised to seek access'** means -
  i. in the case of an application by a local authority, an officer of the local authority or a person authorised by the authority to act on its behalf in connection with the inquiries; or
  ii. in the case of an application by an authorised person, that person.

Ss (3)

Any person:

(a) seeking access to a child in connection with inquiries of a kind mentioned in Sub-section (1); and

(b) purporting to be a person authorised to do so, shall, on being asked to do so, produce some duly authenticated document as evidence that she or he is such a person.

Ss (4)

While an order under this Section - **'an emergency protection order'** - is in force it:

(a) operates as a direction to any person, who is in a position to do so, to comply with any request to produce the child to the applicant;

(b) authorises -
  i. the removal of the child at any time, to accommodation provided by or on behalf of the applicant, and her or his being kept there, or
  ii. the prevention of the child's removal from any hospital, or other place, in which she or he was being accommodated immediately before the making of the order; and

(c) gives the applicant **'parental responsibility'** for the child.

Ss (5)

When an emergency protection order is in force with respect to a child, the applicant:

(a) shall only exercise the power given by virtue of Sub-section (4)(b) in order to safeguard the welfare of the child;

(b) shall take, and shall only take, such action in meeting her or his parental responsibility for the child as is reasonably required to safeguard or promote the welfare of the child (having regard in particular to the duration of the order); and

(c) shall comply with the requirements of any regulations made by the Secretary of State for the purposes of this Sub-section.

Ss (6)

When a court makes an emergency protection order, it may give such directions (if any) as it considers appropriate with respect to:

(a) the contact which is, or is not, to be allowed between the child and any named person;

(b) the medical or psychiatric examination or the assessment of the child.

Ss (7)

When any direction is given under Sub-section (6)(b), the child may, if she or he is of sufficient understanding to make an informed decision, refuse to submit to the examination or other assessment.

Ss (8)

A direction under Sub-section (6)(a) may impose conditions, and one under Sub-section (6)(b) may be to the effect that there is to be:

(a) no such examination or assessment; or

(b) no such examination or assessment unless the court directs otherwise.

Ss (9)

A direction under Sub-section (6) may be:

(a) given when the emergency protection order is made, or at any time while it is in force; and

(b) varied at any time, on the application of any person falling within any class of person prescribed by rules of court for the purposes of this Sub-section.

Ss (10)

When an emergency protection order is in force with respect to a child and:

(a) the applicant has exercised the power given by Sub-section (4)(b)(i), but it appears to her or him that it is safe for the child to be returned; or

(b) the applicant has exercised the power given by Sub-section (4)(b)(ii), but it appears to her or him that it is safe for the child to be allowed to be removed from the place in question;

she or he shall return the child or (as the case may be) allow her or him to be removed.

Ss (11)

If she or he is required by Sub-section (10) to return the child, the applicant shall:

(a) return her or him to the care of the person from whose care she or he was removed; or

(b) if that is not reasonably practicable, return her or him to the care of -
   i. her or his parent, or
   ii. any person who is not a parent of hers or his but who has parental responsibility for her or him, or
   iii. such other person as the applicant (with the agreement of the court) considers appropriate.

Ss (12)

If the applicant has been required by Sub-section (10) to return the child, or to allow her or him to be removed, she or he may again exercise her or his powers with respect to the child (at any time while the emergency protection order remains in force) if it appears to her or him that a change in the circumstances of the case makes it necessary for her or him to do so.

Ss (13)

When an emergency protection order has been made with respect to a child, the applicant shall, subject to any direction given under Sub-section (6), allow the child reasonable contact with:

(a) her or his parents;

(b) any person who is not a parent of hers or his but who has parental responsibility for her or him;

continued overleaf

FIG 2: EMERGENCY PROTECTION ORDERS (EPOs)

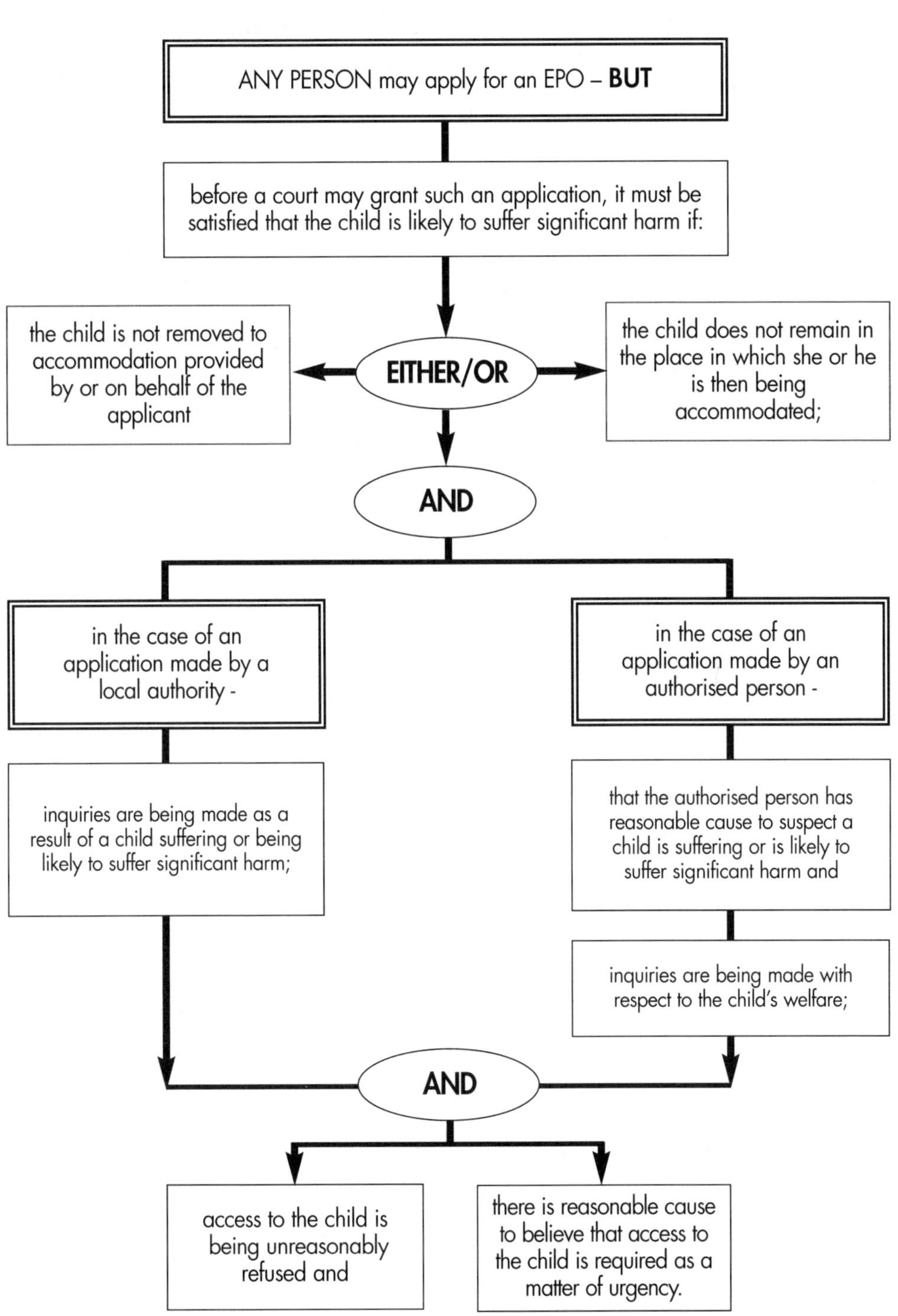

(c) any person with whom she or he was living immediately before the making of the order;

(d) any person in whose favour a contact order is in force with respect to her or him;

(e) any person who is allowed to have contact with the child by virtue of an order under Section 34 (parental contact etc with children in care); and

(f) any person acting on behalf of any of those persons.

Ss (14)

Whenever it is reasonably practicable to do so, an emergency protection order shall name the child; and if it does not name her or him, it shall describe her or him as clearly as possible.

Ss (15)

A person shall be guilty of an offence if she or he intentionally obstructs any person exercising the power under Sub-section (4)(b) to remove, or prevent the removal of, a child.

Ss (16)

A person guilty of an offence under Sub-section (15) shall be liable on summary conviction to a fine not exceeding level 3 on the standard scale (£1,000 at the time of going to press).

Notes

'Significant harm' is defined by Section 31(9) and (10) of this Act as set out in Applications for Care Orders and Supervision Orders (see 2.4b).

An emergency protection order has effect for a maximum of eight days (the duration of the order will be specified by the court). If the last of those eight days is either a Sunday or a Bank Holiday, the court may specify a period which ends at noon on the first later day that is not such a holiday (Section 45(1) and (2) Children Act 1989).

If an emergency protection order is made on an application under Section 46(7) - see 1.1. - the period of eight days above-mentioned shall begin with the first day on which the child was taken into police protection under Section 46, (Section 45(3) Children Act 1989).

2.2a. Power to include exclusion requirements in emergency protection orders

Section 44A Children Act 1989 as inserted by the Family Law Act 1996

Ss (1)

When:

(a) on being satisfied as mentioned in Section 44(1) (a), (b) or (c), the court makes an emergency protection order with respect to a child; and

(b) the conditions mentioned in Sub-section (2) below are satisfied;

the court may include an exclusion requirement in the emergency protection order.

Ss (2)

The conditions are:

(a) that there is reasonable cause to believe that if a person - the **'relevant person'** - is excluded from a dwelling house in which the child lives, then -
   i. in the case of an order made on the grounds mentioned in Section 44(1)(a), the child will not be likely to suffer significant harm, even though the child is not removed as mentioned in Section 44(1)(a)(ii), or
   ii. in the case of an order made on the grounds mentioned in Section 44(1)(b) or (c), the inquiries referred to in that Paragraph will cease to be frustrated; and

(b) that another person living in the dwelling house (whether a parent of the child or some other person) -
   i. is able and willing to give the child the care which it would be reasonable to expect a parent to give her or him, and
   ii. consents to the inclusion of the exclusion requirement.

Ss (3)

For the purposes of this Section, an **'exclusion requirement'** is any one or more of the following:

(a) a provision requiring the relevant person to leave a dwelling house in which she or he is living with the child;

(b) a provision prohibiting the relevant person from entering a dwelling house in which the child lives; and

(c) a provision excluding the relevant person from a defined area in which the dwelling house in which the child lives is situated.

Ss (4)

The court may provide that the exclusion requirement is to have effect for a shorter period than the other provisions of the emergency protection order.

Ss (5)

When the court makes an emergency protection order containing an exclusion requirement, the court may attach a power of arrest to the exclusion requirement.

Ss (6)

When the court attaches a power of arrest to an exclusion requirement of an emergency protection order, it may provide that the power of arrest is to have shorter effect than the exclusion requirement.

Ss (7)

Any period specified for the purposes of Sub-sections (4) or (6) may be extended by the court (on one or more occasions) on an application to vary or discharge the emergency protection order.

Ss (8)

If a power of arrest is attached to the exclusion requirement of an emergency protection order by virtue of Sub-section (5), a constable may arrest without warrant any person whom she or he has reasonable cause to believe to be in breach of the requirement.

Ss (9)

Sections 47(7), (11), (12) and 48 of, and Schedule 5 to, the Family Law Act 1996 shall have effect in relation to a person arrested under Sub-section (8) of this Section as they have effect in relation to a person arrested under Section 47(6)* of that Act.

* Section 47(6) of the Family Law Act 1996 gives a court the authority to attach a power of arrest for breach of an occupation or non-molestation order made under that Act. The Sections and Schedule mentioned above relate to the bringing of the arrested person before the court that made the order within 24 hours (not including Christmas Day, Good Friday or any Sunday) and the power of the court to remand that person.

Ss (10)

If, while an emergency protection order containing an exclusion requirement is in force, the applicant has removed the child from the dwelling house from which the relevant person is excluded to other accommodation for a continuous period of more than 24 hours, the order shall cease to have effect in so far as it imposes the exclusion requirement.

2.2b. Undertakings relating to emergency protection orders

Section 44B Children Act 1989 as inserted by the Family Law Act 1996

Ss (1)

In any case in which the court has the power to include an exclusion requirement in an emergency protection order, the court may accept an undertaking from the relevant person.

Ss (2)

No power of arrest may be attached to any undertaking given under Sub-section (1).

Ss (3)

An undertaking given to a court under Sub-section (1):

(a) shall be enforceable as if it were an order of the court; and

(b) shall cease to have effect if, while it is in force, the applicant has removed the child from the dwelling house from which the relevant person is excluded to other accommodation for a continuous period of more than 24 hours.

2.3. Child assessment orders

Section 43 Children Act 1989

Ss (1)

On the application of a local authority or authorised person for an order to be made under this Section with respect to a child, the court may make an order if, and only if, it is satisfied that:

(a) the applicant has reasonable cause to suspect that the child is suffering, or is likely to suffer, significant harm;

(b) an assessment of the state of the child's health or development, and of the way in which she or he has been treated, is required to enable the applicant to determine whether or not the child is suffering, or is likely to suffer, significant harm; and

(c) it is unlikely that such an assessment will be made, or be satisfactory, in the absence of an order under this Section.

Ss (2)

In this Act a **'child assessment order'** means an order made under this Section.

Ss (3)

A court may treat an application made under this Section as an application for an emergency protection order.

Ss (4)

No court shall make a child assessment order if it is satisfied:

(a) that there are grounds for making an emergency protection order with respect to the child; and

(b) that it ought to make such an order rather than a child assessment order.

Ss (5)

A child assessment order shall:

(a) specify the date by which the assessment is to begin; and

(b) have effect for such period, not exceeding seven days beginning with that date, as may be specified in the order.

Ss (6)

When a child assessment order is in force with respect to a child, it shall be the duty of any person who is in a position to produce the child:

(a) to produce her or him to such a person as may be named in the order; and

(b) to comply with such directions relating to the assessment of the child as the court thinks fit to specify in the order.

Ss (7)

A child assessment order authorises any person to carry out the assessment in accordance with the terms of the order.

Ss (8)

Regardless of Sub-section (7), if the child is of sufficient understanding to make an informed decision, she or he may refuse to submit to a medical or psychiatric examination or other assessment.

Ss (9)

The child may only be kept away from home:

(a) in accordance with directions specified in the order;

(b) if it is necessary for the purposes of the assessment; and

(c) for such period or periods as may be specified in the order.

Ss (10)

If the child is to be kept away from home, the order shall contain such directions as the court thinks fit with regard to the contact that she or he must be allowed to have with other persons while away from home.

Ss (11)

Any person making an application for a child assessment order shall take such steps as are reasonably practicable to ensure that notice of the application is given to:

(a) the child's parents;

(b) any person who is not a parent of hers or his but who has parental responsibility for her or him;

(c) any other person caring for the child;

(d) any person in whose favour a contact order is in force with respect to the child;

(e) any person allowed to have contact with the child by virtue of an order under Section 34 (parental contact with children in care - see 2.4c.i.); and

(f) the child;

before the hearing of the application.

Ss (12)

Rules of court may make provisions as to the circumstances in which:

(a) any of the persons mentioned in Sub-section (11); or

(b) such other persons as may be specified in the rules,

may apply to the court for a child assessment order to be varied or discharged.

Ss (13)

In this Section **'authorised person'** means a person who is an authorised person for the purposes of Section 31 as outlined in S 31(9) (applications for care orders and supervision orders - see 2.4b).

Note

Police officers are not authorised people.

2.4. Care orders and supervision orders

2.4a. Interim care/supervision orders

Section 38 Children Act 1989

Ss (1)

If:

(a) in any proceedings on an application for a care order or supervision order, the proceedings are adjourned; or

(b) the court gives a direction under Section 37(1) (power of a family proceedings court to direct an authority to investigate a child's circumstances),

the court may make an interim care order or an interim supervision order with respect to the child concerned.

Ss (2)

A court shall not make an interim care order or interim supervision order under this Section unless it is satisfied that there are reasonable grounds for believing that the circumstances with respect to the child are as mentioned in Section 31(2) (applications for care orders and supervision orders - see 2.4b).

Ss (3)

If, in any proceedings on an application for a care order or supervision order, a court makes a residence order with respect to the child concerned, it shall also make an interim supervision order with respect to her or him unless satisfied that her or his welfare will be satisfactorily safeguarded without an interim order being made.

Ss (4)

An interim order made under or by virtue of this Section shall have effect for such period as may be specified in the order, but shall in any event cease to have effect on whichever of the following events first occurs:

(a) the expiry of the period of eight weeks beginning with the date on which the order is made;

(b) if the order is the second or subsequent such order made with respect to the same child in the same proceedings - the expiry of the **'relevant period'**;

(c) in a case which falls within Sub-section (1)(a) - the disposal of the application;

(d) in a case which falls within Sub-section (1)(b) - the disposal of an application for a care order or supervision order made by the authority with respect to the child;

(e) in any case which falls within Sub-section (1)(b) in which the court has given a direction under Section 37(4)* - but no application for a care order or supervision order has been made with respect to the child - the expiry of the period fixed by that direction.

* Section 37(4) - power of a family proceedings court to specify the time by which information will be provided to it, following a direction made to an authority to investigate a child's circumstances.

Ss (5)
In Sub-section (4)(b) the **'relevant period'** means:

(a) the period of four weeks beginning with the date on which the order in question is made; or

(b) the period of eight weeks beginning with the date on which the first order was made if that period ends later than the period mentioned in Paragraph (a).

Ss (6)
When the court makes an interim care order, or interim supervision order, it may give such directions as it considers appropriate (if any) with regard to the medical or psychiatric examination or other assessment of the child - but if the child is of sufficient understanding to make an informed decision she or he may refuse to submit to the examination or other assessment.

Ss (7)
A direction under Sub-section (6) may be to the effect that there is to be:

(a) no such examination or assessment; or

(b) no such examination or assessment unless the court directs otherwise.

Ss (8)
A direction under Sub-section (6) may be:

(a) given when the interim order is made, or at any time while it is in force; and

(b) varied at any time on the application of any person falling within any class of person prescribed by rules of court for the purposes of this Sub-section.

Ss (9)
Paragraphs 4 and 5 of Schedule 3* shall not apply in relation to an interim supervision order.

* Paragraphs 4 and 5 of Schedule 3 - power of the court to direct psychiatric and medical examinations/treatment when granting a supervision order.

Ss (10)
When a court makes an order under or by virtue of this Section it shall, in determining the period for which the order is to be in force, consider whether any party who was or might have been opposed to the making of the order, was in a position to argue her or his case in full.

2.4a.i. Power to include exclusion requirements in interim care order

Section 38A Children Act 1989 as inserted by the Family Law Act 1996

Ss (1)
When:

(a) on being satisfied that there are reasonable grounds for believing that the circumstances with respect to a child are as mentioned in Section 31(2)(a) and (b)(i) Children Act 1989 (see 2.4b), the court makes an interim care order with respect to a child; and

(b) the conditions mentioned in Sub-section (2) below are satisfied;

the court may include an exclusion requirement in the interim care order.

Ss (2)
The conditions are:

(a) that there is reasonable cause to believe that if a person - the **'relevant person'** - is excluded from a dwelling house in which the child lives, the child will cease to suffer or cease to be likely to suffer significant harm; and

(b) that another person living in the dwelling house (whether a parent of the child or some other person) -
   i. is able and willing to give the child the care which it would be reasonable to expect a parent to give her or him; and
   ii. consents to the inclusion of the exclusion requirement.

Ss (3)
For the purposes of this Section, an exclusion requirement is any one or more of the following:

(a) a provision requiring the relevant person to leave a dwelling house in which she or he is living with the child;

(b) a provision prohibiting the relevant person from entering a dwelling house in which the child lives; and

(c) a provision excluding the relevant person from a defined area in which the dwelling house in which the child lives is situated.

Ss (4)
The court may provide that the exclusion requirement is to have effect for a shorter period than the other provisions of the interim care order.

Ss (5)
When the court makes an interim care order containing an exclusion requirement, the court may attach a power of arrest to the exclusion requirement.

Ss (6)
When the court attaches a power of arrest to an exclusion requirement of an interim care order, it may provide that the power of arrest is to have shorter effect than the exclusion requirement.

Ss (7)
Any period specified for the purposes of Sub-sections (4) or (6) may be extended by the court (on one or more occasions) on an application to vary or discharge the interim care order.

Ss (8)
When a power of arrest is attached to the exclusion requirement of an interim care order by virtue of Sub-section (5), a constable may arrest without warrant any person whom she or he has reasonable cause to believe to be in breach of the requirement.

Ss (9)
Sections 47(7), (11), (12) and 48 of, and Schedule 5 to, the Family Law Act 1996* shall have effect in relation to a person arrested under Sub-section (8) of this Section as they have effect in relation to a person arrested under Section 47(6)** of that Act.

* The Sections and Schedule mentioned above relate to the bringing of the arrested person before the court that made the order within 24 hours (not including Christmas Day, Good Friday or any Sunday) and the power of the court to remand that person).

** Section 47(6) of the Family Law Act 1996 gives a court the authority to attach a power of arrest for breach of an occupation or non-molestation order made under that Act.

Ss (10)
If, while an interim care order containing an exclusion requirement is in force, the applicant has removed the child from the dwelling house from which the relevant person is excluded to other accommodation for a continuous period of more than 24 hours, the order shall cease to have effect in so far as it imposes the exclusion requirement.

2.4a.ii. Undertakings relating to interim care orders

Section 38B Children Act 1989 as inserted by the Family Law Act 1996

Ss (1)
In any case in which the court has the power to include an exclusion requirement in an interim care order, the court may accept an undertaking from the relevant person.

Ss (2)
No power of arrest may be attached to any undertaking given under Sub-section (1).

Ss (3)
An undertaking given to a court under Sub-section (1):

(a) shall be enforceable as if it were an order of the court; and

(b) shall cease to have effect if, while it is in force, the applicant has removed the child from the dwelling house from which the relevant person is excluded to other accommodation for a continuous period of more than 24 hours.

2.4b. Applications for care orders and supervision orders

Section 31 Children Act 1989

Ss (1)
On the application of any local authority or **'authorised person'**, the court may make an order:

(a) placing the child - with respect to whom the application is made - in the care of a designated local authority; or

(b) putting her or him under the supervision of a designated local authority or of a probation officer.

Ss (2)

A court may only make a care order or supervision order if it is satisfied:

(a) that the child concerned is suffering, or is likely to suffer, **'significant harm'**; and

(b) that the harm, or likelihood of harm, is attributable to -

i. the care given to the child - or likely to be given to her or him if the order were not made - not being what it would be reasonable to expect a parent to give to her or him, or

ii. the child's being beyond parental control.

Ss (3)

No care order or supervision order may be made with respect to a child who has reached the age of 17 years (or 16 years in the case of a child who is married).

Ss (4)

An application under this Section may be made on its own or in any other family proceedings.

Ss (5)

The court may:

(a) on an application for a care order, make a supervision order;

(b) on an application for a supervision order, make a care order.

Ss (6)

When an authorised person proposes to make an application under this Section she or he shall:

(a) if it is reasonably practicable to do so; and

(b) before making the application,

consult the local authority in whose area the child concerned is ordinarily resident.

Ss (7)

An application by an authorised person shall not be entertained by the court if, at the time when it is made, the child concerned is:

(a) the subject of an earlier application for a care order or supervision order which has not been disposed of; or

(b) subject to -

i. an existing care order or supervision order,

ii. an order made under Section 7(7)(b)* of the Children and Young Persons Act 1969,

iii. a supervision requirement within the meaning of the Social Work (Scotland) Act 1968.

* Section 7(7)(b) - power of the court to make a supervision order if a child or young person is convicted of an offence.

Ss (8)

The local authority designated in a care order must be:

(a) the authority within whose area the child is ordinarily resident; or

(b) if the child does not reside in the area of a local authority, the authority within whose area any circumstances arose in consequence of which the order is being made.

Ss (9)

In this Section:

'Authorised person' means:

(a) the National Society for the Prevention of Cruelty to Children and any of its officers; and

(b) any person authorised by the Secretary of State to bring proceedings under this Section - and any officer of a body which is so authorised **(this does not include the police)**.

'Harm' means ill-treatment or the impairment of health and development. **'Development'** means physical, intellectual, emotional, social or behavioural development. **'Health'** means physical or mental health. **'Ill-treatment'** includes sexual abuse and forms of ill-treatment which are not physical.

Ss (10)
If the question of whether harm suffered by a child is **'significant'** turns on the child's health or development, her or his health or development shall be compared with that which could reasonably be expected of a similar child.

Ss (11)
In this Act **'care order'*** means an order made under Sub-section (1)(a) and, except where express provision to the contrary is made, includes an interim care order made under Section 38 of this Act.

* The above is subject to Section 105(1) - interpretation of the terms in the Children Act 1989. This extends the definition of care order to orders made under other enactments which are deemed to be or have the effect of care orders under this Act.

'Supervision order' means an order under Sub-section (1)(b) and, except where express provision to the contrary is made, includes an interim supervision order made under Section 38.

2.4b.i. Period within which applications for care orders and supervision orders must be disposed of

Section 32 Children Act 1989

Ss (1)
A court hearing an application for an order under this part shall - in the light of any rules made by virtue of Sub-section (2):

(a) draw up a timetable with a view to disposing of the application without delay; and

(b) give such directions as it considers appropriate for the purpose of ensuring, so far as is reasonable practicable, that the timetable is adhered to.

Ss (2)
Rules of the court may:

(a) specify periods within which specified steps must be taken in relation to such proceedings; and

(b) make other provision with respect to such proceedings for the purpose of ensuring, so far as reasonably practicable, that they are disposed of without delay.

2.4c. The effect of care orders

Section 33 Children Act 1989

Ss (1)
When a care order is made with respect to a child it shall be the duty - of the local authority designated by the order - to receive the child into its care and to keep her or him in its care while the order remains in force.

Ss (2)
If:

(a) a care order has been made with respect to a child on the application of an authorised person; but

(b) the local authority designated by the order was not informed that that person proposed to make the application;

the child may be kept in the care of that person until received into the care of the authority.

Ss (3)
While the care order is in force with respect to a child, the local authority designated by the order shall:

(a) have parental responsibility for the child; and

(b) have the power (subject to the following provisions of this Section) to determine the extent to which a parent or guardian of the child may meet her or his parental responsibility for the child.

Ss (4)
The authority may not exercise the power in Sub-section 3(b) unless it is satisfied that it is necessary to do so in order to safeguard or promote the child's welfare.

Ss (5)
Nothing in Sub-section 3(b) shall prevent a parent or guardian of the child - who has care of her or him - from doing what is reasonable in all the circumstances of the case for the purpose of safeguarding or promoting the child's welfare.

Ss (6)
While a care order is in force with respect to a child, the local authority designated by the order shall:

(a) not cause the child to be brought up in any religious persuasion other than that in which she or he would have been brought up if the order had not been made; or

(b) not have the right -
   i. to consent or refuse to consent to the making of an application with respect to the child under Section 18 of the Adoption Act 1976,
   ii. to agree to or refuse to agree to the making of an adoption order, or an order under Section 55 of the Act of 1976, with respect to the child, or
   iii. to appoint a guardian for the child.

Ss (7)

While a care order is in force with respect to a child, no person may:

(a) cause the child to be known by a new surname; or

(b) remove her or him from the United Kingdom;

without either the written consent of every person who has parental responsibility for the child, or the leave of the court.

Ss (8)

Sub-section (7)(b) does not:

(a) prevent the removal of such a child, for a period of less than one month, by the authority in whose care she or he is; or

(b) apply to arrangements for such a child to live outside England and Wales which are governed by Paragraph 19 of Schedule 2*.

* Schedule 2 - local authority's duty to apply for the approval of the court if they want to arrange or assist in arranging a child in care to live outside England and Wales.

Ss (9)

The power in Sub-section (3)(b) is subject - in addition to being subject to the provisions of this Section - to any right, duty, power, responsibility or authority which a parent or guardian of the child has in relation to the child and the child's property by virtue of any other enactment.

2.4c.i. Parental contact etc with children in care

Section 34 Children Act 1989

Ss (1)

When a child is in the care of a local authority, the authority shall (subject to the provisions of this Section) allow the child reasonable contact with:

(a) her or his parents;

(b) any guardian of hers or his;

(c) - in cases in which there was a residence order in force with respect to the child immediately before the care order was made - the person in whose favour the order was made; and

(d) - in cases in which, immediately before the care order was made, a person had the care of the child by virtue of an order made in the exercise of the High Court's inherent jurisdiction with respect to children - that person.

Ss (2)

On application made by the authority or the child, the court may make such an order as it considers appropriate with respect to the contact which is to be allowed between the child and any named person.

Ss (3)

On an application made by:

(a) any person mentioned in Paragraphs (a) to (d) of Sub-section (1); or

(b) any person who has obtained the leave of the court to make the application;

the court may make such order as it considers appropriate with respect to the contact which is to be allowed between the child and that person.

Ss (4)

On an application made by the authority or the child, the court may make an order authorising the authority to refuse to allow contact between the child and any person who is mentioned in Paragraphs (a) to (d) of Sub-section (1), and named in the order.

Ss (5)
When making a care order with respect to a child, or in any family proceedings in connection with a child who is in the care of a local authority - the court may make an order under this Section - even though no application for such an order has been made with respect to the child - if it considers that the order should be made.

Ss (6)
An authority may refuse to allow contact that would otherwise be required by virtue of Sub-section (1) or an order under this Section if:

(a) it is satisfied that it is necessary to do so in order to safeguard or promote the child's welfare; and

(b) the refusal -
i. is decided upon as a matter of urgency, and
ii. does not last for more than seven days.

Ss (7)
An order under this Section may impose such conditions as the court considers appropriate.

Ss (8)
The Secretary of State may, by regulation, make provision as to:

(a) the steps to be taken by a local authority which has exercised its powers under Sub-section (6);

(b) the circumstances in which, and conditions subject to which, the terms of any order under this Section may be departed from, by agreement between the local authority and the person in relation to whom this order is made;

(c) notification, by a local authority, of any variation or suspension of arrangements made (otherwise than under an order under this Section) with a view to affording any person contact with a child to whom this Section applies.

Ss (9)
The court may vary or discharge any order made under this Section - on the application of the authority, the child concerned or the person named in the order.

Ss (10)
An order under this Section may be made either at the same time as the care order itself or later.

Ss (11)
Before making a care order with respect to any child, the court shall:

(a) consider the arrangements which the authority has made, or proposes to make, for affording any person contact with the child to whom this Section applies; and

(b) invite the parties to the proceedings to comment on those arrangements.

2.4d. Supervision orders

Section 35 Children Act 1989

Ss (1)
While a supervision order is in force, it shall be the duty of the supervisor:

(a) to advise, assist and befriend the supervised child;

(b) to take such steps as are reasonably necessary to give effect to the order; and

(c) in cases in which -
i. the order is not wholly complied with, or
ii. the supervisor considers that the order may no longer be necessary;

to consider whether or not to apply to the court for its variation or discharge.

2.5. Residence, contact and other orders

Section 8(1) and (2) Children Act 1989

2.5a. Section 8 orders

A Section 8 order includes any of the following:

'Contact order' - This order requires the person with whom a child is living, or a person with whom a child is going to live, to allow the child to visit or to stay with the person named in the order, or to otherwise allow for that person and the child to have contact with each other.

'Prohibited steps order' - This order means that no step - which could be taken by a parent in meeting her or his parental responsibility for a child, and which is of a kind specified in the order - shall be taken by any person without the consent of the court.

'Residence order' - This refers to an order settling the arrangements to be made in respect of the person with whom the child is to live.

'Specific issue order' - This is an order giving directions for the purpose of determining a specific question which has arisen, or which may arise, in connection with any aspect of parental responsibility for a child.

2.5b. Applications for Section 8 orders

Section 10 Children Act 1989

Ss (1)

In any family proceedings in which a question arises with respect to the welfare of any child, the court may make a Section 8 order with respect to the child if:

(a) an application for the order has been made by a person who -
   i. is entitled to apply for a Section 8 order with respect to the child, or
   ii. has obtained the leave of the court to make the application; or

(b) the court considers that the order should be made even though no such application has been made.

Ss (2)

The court may also make a Section 8 order with respect to any child, on the application of a person who:

(a) is entitled to apply for a Section 8 order with respect to the child; or

(b) has obtained the leave of the court to make the application.

Ss (3)

This Section is subject to the restrictions imposed by Section 9 (see facing page).

Ss (4)

The following persons are **'entitled to apply'** for any Section 8 order with respect to a child:

(a) any parent* or guardian of the child -

* parent would include a putative father without parental responsibility, but not a natural parent who has lost parenthood through adoption or an order freeing the child for adoption;

(b) any person in whose favour a residence order is in force with respect to the child.

Ss (5)

The following persons are **'entitled to apply'** for a residence or contact order with respect to a child;

(a) any party to a marriage - whether or not subsisting - in relation to whom the child is a child of the family;

(b) any person with whom the child has lived for a period of at least three years** -

** this period need not be continuous but must not have begun more than five years before or ended more than three months before the making of the application;

(c) any person whom -
   i. in any case in which a residence order is in force with respect to the child - has the consent of each of the persons in whose favour the order was made,
   ii. in any case in which the child is in the care of a local authority - has the consent of that authority,
   iii. in any other case - has the consent of each of those (if any) who have parental responsibility for the child.

Ss (6)

Any person - who would not otherwise be entitled to apply for a variation or discharge of a Section 8 order by virtue of Sub-sections (4) and (5) (above) - shall be so entitled if:

(a) the order was made on her or his application; or

(b) in the case of a contact order, she or he is mentioned in the order.

Ss (7)

Any person, who falls within a category of person prescribed by rules of court, is entitled to apply for such a Section 8 order as may be prescribed in relation to that category of person.

Ss (8)

When the person applying for leave to make an application for a Section 8 order is the child concerned, the court may only grant leave if it is satisfied that she or he has sufficient understanding to make the proposed application for the Section 8 order.

Ss (9)

When the person applying for leave to make an application for a Section 8 order is not the child concerned, the court shall, in deciding whether or not to grant leave, have particular regard to:

(a) the nature of the proposed application for the Section 8 order;

(b) the applicant's connection with the child;

(c) any risk there might be of that proposed application disrupting the child's life to the extent that she or he would be harmed by it; and

(d) in cases in which the child is being looked after by a local authority -
i. the authority's plans for the child's future, and
ii. the wishes and feelings of the child's parents.

2.5c. Restrictions on making Section 8 orders

Section 9 Children Act 1989

Ss (1)

No court shall make any Section 8 order, other than a residence order, with respect to a child who is in the care of a local authority.

Ss (2)

No application may be made by a local authority for a residence order or a contact order and no court shall make such an order in favour of a local authority.

Ss (3)

A person who is, or was at any time in the last six months, a local authority foster parent of a child, may not apply for leave to apply for a Section 8 order with respect to a child unless:

(a) she or he has the consent of that authority;

(b) she or he is a relative of the child; or

(c) the child has lived with her or him for at least three years preceding the application.

Ss (4)

The period of three years mentioned in Subsection (3)(c) need not be continuous but must have begun not more than five years before the making of the application.

Ss (5)

No court shall exercise its powers to make a specific issue order or prohibited steps order:

(a) with a view to achieving a result which could be achieved by making a residence or contact order; or

(b) in any way which is denied to the High Court - by Section 100(2) Children Act 1989 - in the exercise of its inherent jurisdiction with respect to children.

Ss (6)

No court shall make any Section 8 order which is to have effect for a period which will end after the child has reached the age of 16 years - unless it is satisfied that the circumstances of the case are exceptional.

Ss (7)

No court shall make any Section 8 order - other than one varying or discharging such an order - with respect to a child who has reached the age of 16 years - unless it is satisfied that the circumstances of the case are exceptional.

PART TWO

OFFENCES

CHAPTER 3

OFFENCES INVOLVING INDECENCY

3.1. Rape

> It is an offence for a man to rape a woman or another man.
>
> Section 1(1) Sexual Offences Act 1956 (as amended by Section 142 of the Criminal Justice and Public Order Act 1994)

Notes

For the purposes of this offence, **'man'** includes **'boy'** (Section 46 Sexual Offences Act 1956).

By virtue of Section 1 of the Sexual Offences Act 1993, a boy under 14 years of age (although not under 10 years since the age of criminal responsibility is unaffected by this enactment) may be convicted of rape in respect of offences committed on or after 20.9.93.

A boy under 14 cannot be convicted of rape in respect of offences committed before this date by virtue of case law dating back to 1836 (*R v Groombridge*).

A man commits **'rape'** if:

a. he has sexual intercourse with a person (whether vaginal or anal) who at the time of the intercourse does not consent to it; and

b. at the time he knows that the person does not consent to the intercourse or he is reckless as to whether that person consents to it;

(Section 1(2) Sexual Offences Act 1956 (as amended by Section 142 of the Criminal Justice and Public Order Act 1994)).

'Sexual intercourse' means penetration (however slight) of the vagina or anus by the penis. Ejaculation does not necessarily have to take place (Section 44 Sexual Offences Act 1956).

'Consent' should be given its ordinary meaning (Richardson 1998). While every consent involves a submission it does not follow that every submission involves consent (*R v Larter and Castleton* 1995 Crim LR 75 CA as cited in Draycott and Carr 1998).

- The consent of a girl under 13 years of age is no defence to a charge under Section 5 of this Act – Unlawful Sexual Intercourse with a Girl Under 13 Years (see 3.5).
- Except in specific circumstances in which the defendant is married to the alleged victim, the consent of a girl under 16 years of age is no defence to a charge under Section 6 of this Act – Unlawful Sexual Intercourse with a Girl Under 16 years (see 3.6).
- Except in specific circumstances in which the defendant is married to the alleged victim, the consent of a girl under 16 years of age is no defence to a charge under Section 14 of this Act – Indecent Assault on a Woman (see 3.16).
- The consent of a boy under 16 years of age is no defence to a charge under Section 15 of this Act – Indecent Assault on a Man (see 3.17).
- A jury, on acquitting on a charge of rape in which the alleged victim was a girl under 16 years of age, may convict on an indecent assault under Section 14 of this Act (see 3.16) (*R v Hodgson* 1973 2 All ER 552).
- The consent of a person under 16 years of age is no defence to a charge of buggery under Section 12 of this Act (see 3.13).

The provisions for the anonymity of alleged victims to this offence are contained within Section 4 Sexual Offences (Amendment) Act 1976.

Punishable

on indictment with life imprisonment.

3.2. Procurement of a woman by threats

> It is an offence for a person to procure a woman - by threats or intimidation - to have sexual intercourse in any part of the world.
>
> Section 2(1) Sexual Offences Act 1956

Notes

'Woman' includes **'girl'** for the purposes of this offence (Section 46 Sexual Offences Act 1956).

'Sexual intercourse' has the same meaning as in Rape (previous page).

The provisions for the anonymity of alleged victims to this offence are contained within Section 1 Sexual Offences (Amendment) Act 1992.

Example

This offence might be charged if a child is threatened so as to force her to go overseas for the purpose of sexual intercourse (see also 3.7 - Section 23 Sexual Offences Act 1956).

Punishable

on indictment with two years' imprisonment.

3.3. Procurement of a woman by false pretences

> It is an offence for a person to procure a woman - by false pretences or false representations - to have sexual intercourse in any part of the world.
>
> Section 3(1) Sexual Offences Act 1956

Notes

'Woman' includes **'girl'** for the purposes of this offence (Section 46 Sexual Offences Act 1956).

In the case of **'false pretences'** a false promise will not be sufficient. There must be a misrepresentation of an existing fact (*R v Williams* 1923 1 KB 340).

'Sexual intercourse' has the same meaning as in Rape (see 3.1).

The provisions for the anonymity of alleged victims to this offence are contained within Section 1 Sexual Offences (Amendment) Act 1992.

Example

A charge under this Section might be considered if a child is told lies in order to secure her compliance for the purpose of sending her overseas to take part in unlawful sexual intercourse (see also 3.7 - Section 23 Sexual Offences Act 1956).

Punishable

on indictment with two years' imprisonment.

3.4. Administering drugs to obtain or facilitate intercourse

> It is an offence for a person to apply, administer to, or cause to be taken by, a woman - any drug, matter or thing - with intent to stupefy or overpower her so as to enable any man to have unlawful sexual intercourse with her.
>
> Section 4 (1) Sexual Offences Act 1956

Notes

'Woman' includes **'girl'** for the purposes of this offence (Section 46 Sexual Offences Act 1956).

'Thing' might include intoxicating liquor, provided that the necessary intent can be established (Draycott and Carr 1998).

'Unlawful' means outside marriage (*R v Chapman* 1959 3 All ER 143).

'Sexual intercourse' has the same meaning as in Rape - see 3.1.

The provisions for the anonymity of alleged victims to this offence are contained within Section 1 Sexual Offences (Amendment) Act 1992.

Example

This offence might be charged if a girl or young woman is given alcohol or drugs for the purposes of securing her compliance to unlawful sexual intercourse. If intercourse actually takes place as a result of the administration of drugs or alcohol, it may be possible to argue that a rape has taken place given that consent has not freely been given. This is particularly so if the girl or woman concerned is rendered unconscious as a result of the alcohol or drugs (*R v Camplin* 1845, 9 JP424)).

Punishable

on indictment with two years' imprisonment.

3.5. Sexual intercourse with a girl under 13 years

> It is an offence for a man to have unlawful sexual intercourse with a girl under the age of 13 years.
>
> Section 5 Sexual Offences Act 1956

Notes

'Man' includes **'boy'** (Section 46 Sexual Offences Act 1956).

'Unlawful' has the same meaning as in 'Administering Drugs to Obtain or Facilitate Intercourse' (previous page).

'Sexual intercourse' has the same meaning as in Rape - see 3.1).

The girl's consent to the intercourse is no defence (*R v Beale*, 1865 LR 1 CCR 10).

The provisions for the anonymity of alleged victims to this offence are contained within Section 1 Sexual Offences (Amendment) Act 1992.

Example

This offence may be charged if sexual intercourse has taken place but it is not possible to fulfil the elements required to support a charge of rape. Specifically, while the consent of the girl is no defence to this particular charge, it would be necessary to prove that the offence was committed against her will to support a charge of rape.

Punishable

on indictment with life imprisonment (or seven years for an attempt).

3.6. Sexual intercourse with a girl under 16 years

> It is an offence - subject to the exceptions mentioned in this Section - for a man to have unlawful sexual intercourse with a girl under the age of 16 years.
>
> Section 6 Sexual Offences Act 1956

Notes

If a marriage is invalid because the wife is a girl under the age of 16 years, the husband will not be guilty of an offence under this Section provided he genuinely believes her to be his wife and has reasonable grounds for such a belief (Section 6(2) Sexual Offences Act 1956).

In these circumstances, a man married to a girl under 16 years according to foreign law should not be prosecuted for this offence (*Mohammed v Knott* 1969 2 All ER 563).

A man is not guilty of an offence under this Section because he has unlawful sexual intercourse with a girl under the age of 16 years, if he is under the age of 24 years - and has not previously been charged with a like offence - and he believes her to be of the age of 16 years or over - and has reasonable cause for this belief.

'Like offence' means any offence contrary to this Section of the Act, any attempt to commit an offence contrary to this Section of the Act, and an offence contrary to Section 5(1) Criminal Law

Amendment Act 1885 in Scotland (Section 6(3) Sexual Offences Act 1956).

'Charged' means charged before a court having jurisdiction to determine the matter (*R v Rider* 1954 1 All ER 5).

A prosecution for this offence may not be commenced more than 12 months after the alleged offence was committed (Part 2 of Schedule 2 Sexual Offences Act 1956).

'Man' includes **'boy'** (Section 46 Sexual Offences Act 1956).

'Unlawful' has the same meaning as in Administering Drugs to Obtain or Facilitate Intercourse (see 3.4).

'Sexual intercourse' has the same meaning as in Rape (see 3.1).

The provisions for the anonymity of alleged victims to this offence are contained within Section 1 Sexual Offences (Amendment) Act 1992.

Example

As in Section 5 (previous page), this offence may be charged if sexual intercourse has taken place but it is not possible to fulfil the elements required to support a charge of rape. Specifically, while the consent of the girl is no defence to this particular charge, it would be necessary to prove that the offence was committed against her will to support a charge of rape.

Punishable

on indictment with two years' imprisonment.

3.7. Procurement of a girl under 21 years for the purposes of unlawful sexual intercourse

> It is an offence for a person to procure a girl under the age of 21 years to have unlawful sexual intercourse - in any part of the world - with a third person.
>
> Section 23 Sexual Offences Act 1956

Notes

'Unlawful' has the same meaning as in Administering Drugs to Obtain or Facilitate Intercourse (see 3.4).

'Sexual intercourse' has the same meaning as in Rape (see 3.1).

This offence may be charged only if the unlawful sexual intercourse actually takes place. Otherwise, a charge of attempting to commit this offence should be considered (*R v Johnson* 1963, 3 All ER 577).

Example

A charge under this Section might be considered if a child or young person is sent overseas in order to have unlawful sexual intercourse irrespective of whether threats and intimidation (Section 2 Sexual Offences Act 1956 - see 3.2) or false pretenses (Section 3 Sexual Offences Act 1956 - see 3.3) are involved.

Punishable

on indictment with two years' imprisonment.

3.8. Intercourse with a defective

> It is an offence, subject to the exception mentioned below, for a man to have unlawful sexual intercourse with a woman who is a defective.
>
> Section 7 Sexual Offences Act 1956 as substituted by Mental Health Act 1959

Notes

A man is not guilty of an offence under this Section if he does not know or has no reason to suspect the woman to be a defective (Section 7 (2) Sexual Offences Act 1956).

For the purposes of this offence, **'woman'** includes **'girl'** and **'man'** includes **'boy'** (Section 46 Sexual Offences Act 1956).

'Unlawful' has the same meaning as in Administering Drugs to Obtain or Facilitate Intercourse (see 3.4).

'Sexual intercourse' has the same meaning as in Rape (see 3.1).

The unfortunate offensive and rather dated term **'defective'** means a person suffering from a state of arrested or incomplete development of mind which includes severe impairment of intelligence and social functioning within the terms of the Mental Health Act 1959 (Section 45 Sexual Offences Act 1956).

The provisions for the anonymity of alleged victims to this offence are contained within Section 1 Sexual Offences (Amendment) Act 1992.

Punishable

by imprisonment for a maximum of with two years.

3.9. Procurement of a defective

> It is an offence, subject to the exception mentioned below, for a person to procure a woman who is a defective to have unlawful sexual intercourse in any part of the world.
>
> Section 9 Sexual Offences Act 1956

Notes

A person is not guilty of an offence under this Section if she or he does not know or has no reason to suspect the woman to be a defective (Section 9(2) Sexual Offences Act 1956).

For the purposes of this offence, **'woman'** includes **'girl'** and **'man'** includes **'boy'** (Section 46 Sexual Offences Act 1956).

'Unlawful' has the same meaning as in Administering Drugs to Obtain or Facilitate Intercourse (see 3.4).

'Sexual intercourse' has the same meaning as in Rape (see 3.1).

The unfortunate offensive and rather dated term **'defective'** has the same meaning as outlined in Section 7 - see 3.8.

The provisions for the anonymity of alleged victims to this offence are contained within Section 1 Sexual Offences (Amendment) Act 1992.

Punishable

by imprisonment for a maximum of with two years.

3.10. Incest by a man

> It is an offence for a man to have sexual intercourse with a woman he knows to be his grand-daughter, daughter, sister or mother.
>
> Section 10 Sexual Offences Act 1956

Notes

'Sexual intercourse' and **'man'** have the same meaning as in Rape (see 3.1).

'Sister' includes half-sister.

For the purposes of this Section any expression signifying a relationship between two people shall be taken to apply whether or not the relationship can be traced through lawful wedlock.

The provisions for the anonymity of alleged victims to this offence are contained within Section 1 Sexual Offences (Amendment) Act 1992.

Punishable

on indictment with life imprisonment if the girl is under 13 years of age - otherwise with seven years' imprisonment. An attempt is punishable on indictment with seven years' imprisonment if the girl is under 13 years - otherwise an attempt is punishable with two years' imprisonment.

3.11. Incest by a woman

> It is an offence for a woman of 16 years or over to permit a man whom she knows to be her grandfather, father, brother or son to have sexual intercourse with her by her consent.
>
> Section 11 Sexual Offences Act 1956

Notes

'Sexual intercourse' and **'man'** have the same meaning as in Rape (see 3.1).

'Brother' includes half brother.

For the purposes of this Section any expression signifying a relationship between two people shall be taken to apply whether or not the relationship can be traced through lawful wedlock.

The provisions for the anonymity of alleged victims to this offence are contained within Section 1 Sexual Offences (Amendment) Act 1992.

Punishable

on indictment with seven years' imprisonment. An attempt is punishable on indictment with two years' imprisonment.

3.12. Incitement to commit incest by a man

> It is an offence for a man to incite to have sexual intercourse with him - a girl under the age of 16 years - whom he knows to be his grand-daughter, daughter or sister.
>
> Section 54 Criminal Law Act 1977

Notes

'Sexual intercourse' and **'man'** have the same meaning as in Rape (see 3.1).

'Sister' includes half-sister.

For the purposes of this Section any expression signifying a relationship between two people shall be taken to apply whether or not the relationship can be traced through lawful wedlock.

The provisions for the anonymity of alleged victims to this offence are contained within Section 1 Sexual Offences (Amendment) Act 1992.

Punishable

on indictment with two years' imprisonment.

3.13. Buggery

> It is an offence for a person to commit buggery with another person - in circumstances other than those described below - or with an animal.
>
> Section 12(1) Sexual Offences Act 1956

Notes

'Buggery' means penetration of the anus by the penis.

The act of buggery will not be an offence if it takes place in private - provided both parties have both attained the age of 16 years. The responsibility for proving that the act took place other than in private - or that one of the parties was under 16 years - rests with the prosecution (Section 12(1A) and (1C) Sexual Offences Act 1956, as amended by the Police and Criminal Evidence Act 1984, the Criminal Justice and Public Order Act 1994 and the Sexual Offences (Amendment) Act 2000).

A person under the age of 16 does not commit this offence if the other person involved is aged 16 or over. In these circumstances, the offence is only committed by the person who is aged 16 or over.

The act of buggery will not be regarded as being in private if more than two persons take part or are present, or if done in a lavatory to which the public have access (on payment or otherwise) (Section 12(1B) Sexual Offences Act 1956 as amended by the Police and Criminal Evidence Act 1984 and the Criminal Justice and Public Order Act 1994).

In the absence of consent, the more appropriate charge to an act of buggery is likely to be rape (3.1).

The provisions for the anonymity of alleged victims to this offence are contained within Section 1 Sexual Offences (Amendment) Act 1992.

Punishable

on indictment:

a. with life imprisonment if with person aged under 16 years, or with an animal;
b. if the offender is 21 years or over, and the other party is under 18, five years' imprisonment - otherwise, two years' imprisonment.

FIG 3: OFFENCES IN RESPECT OF VAGINAL SEXUAL INTERCOURSE

see Rape (p27) and Buggery (facing page) in respect of anal intercourse

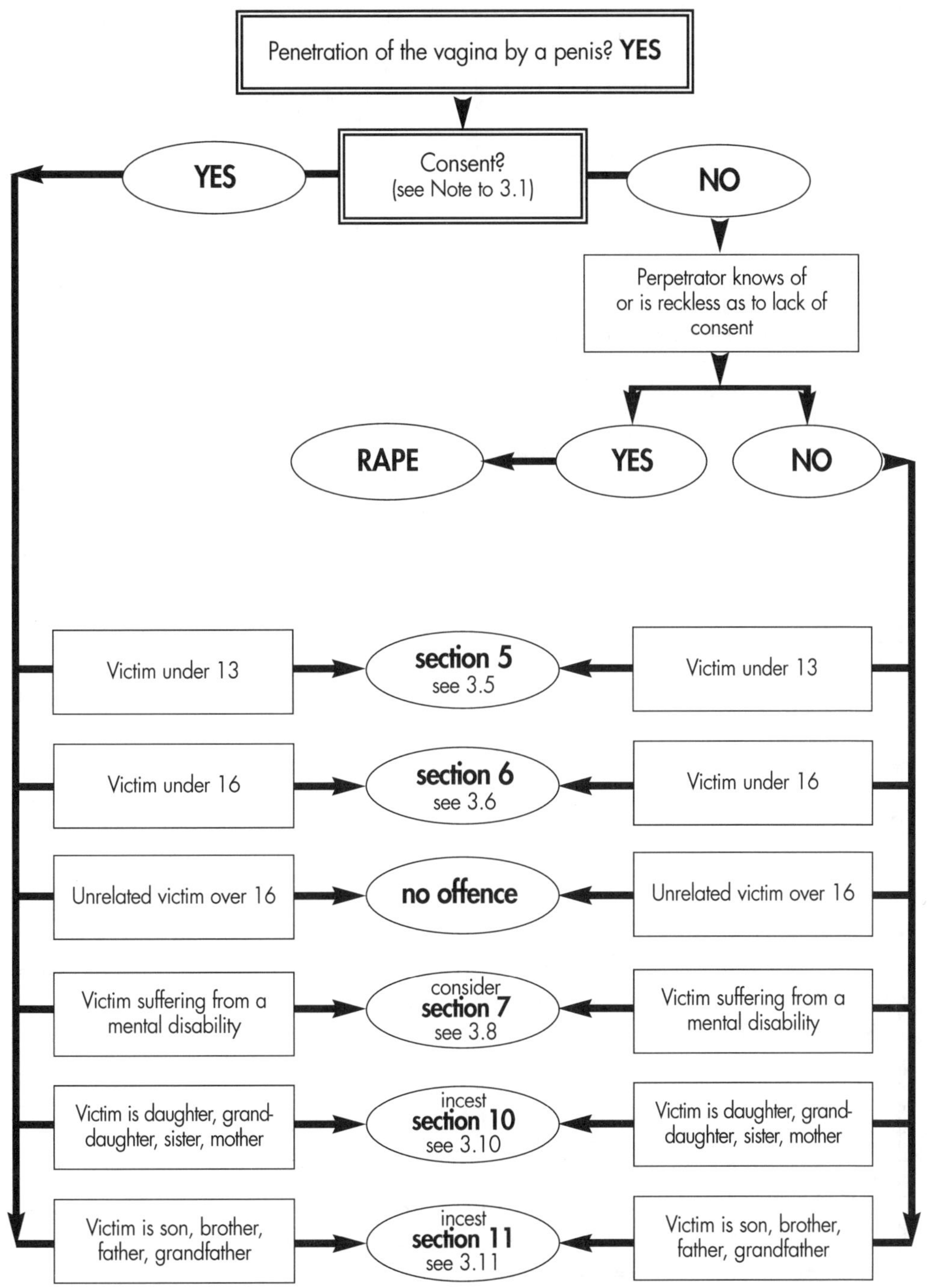

3.14. Assault with intent to commit buggery

> It is an offence for a person to assault another person with intent to commit buggery.
>
> Section 16 Sexual Offences Act 1956

Notes

An **'assault'** is committed by a person who intentionally (or possibly recklessly) causes another person to fear the immediate and unlawful application of force to her or his person - provided that the person making such a threat has the present ability to effect her or his purpose. An assault becomes a battery if unlawful force is actually applied.

'Buggery' means penetration of the anus by the penis.

The provisions for the anonymity of alleged victims to this offence are contained within Section 1 Sexual Offences (Amendment) Act 1992.

Example

This offence might be charged in circumstances in which an assault has taken place with a view to committing buggery, but when the actions of the accused fall short of those necessary to support a charge of attempted rape.

Punishable

on indictment with 10 years' imprisonment.

3.15. Indecency between men

> It is an offence for a man to commit an act of gross indecency with another man - whether in public or private - or to be a party to the commission by a man of an act of gross indecency with another man - or to procure the commission by a man of an act of gross indecency with another man.
>
> Section 13 Sexual Offences Act 1956

Notes

'Man' includes **'boy'** (Section 46 Sexual Offences Act 1956).

An act of gross indecency will not be an offence if it takes place in private, provided both parties have consented and have attained the age of 16 years (S 1(1) Sexual Offences Act 1967 as amended by the Criminal Justice and Public Order Act 1994 and the Sexual Offences (Amendment) Act 2000)

Such an act will not be regarded as being in private if more than two persons take part or are present - or if done in a lavatory to which the public have access (on payment or otherwise),
(S 1(2) Sexual Offences Act 1967 as amended by the Criminal Justice and Public Order Act 1994).

The responsibility for proving that the act took place other than in private, without consent, or that one of the parties was under 16, rests with the prosecution (S 1(6) Sexual Offences Act, 1967 as amended by and the Sexual Offences (Amendment) Act, 2000).

A person under the age of 16 does not commit this offence if the other person involved is aged 16 or over. In these circumstances, the offence is only committed by the person who is aged 16 or over.

Example

This offence might be charged if the actions took place in public with the consent of those involved.

Punishable

on indictment, in circumstances in which the offender is of or over 21 years of age and the other is under 16 years of age, with five years' imprisonment. Otherwise, two years' inprisonment.

3.16. Indecent assault on a woman

> It is an offence (except in the circumstances attributed to Section 14(3) Sexual Offences Act 1956 as outlined below) for a person to make an indecent assault on a woman.
>
> Section 14(1) Sexual Offences Act 1956

Notes

'Indecent assault' requires that an assault of a sexual nature must take place.

'Assault' has the same meaning as in Assault with Intent to Commit Buggery (see 3.14). The assault must be either inherently indecent or capable of being indecent and must be accompanied by an indecent motive.

'Woman' includes **'girl'** (Section 46 Sexual Offences Act 1956).

A girl under 16 years of age cannot give consent to an assault under this Section (S 14(2) Sexual Offences Act 1956). If the girl is under 13 years this should be stated on the indictment (*Draycott and Carr* 1998).

If a marriage is invalid because the wife is a girl under the age of 16 years, the husband will not be guilty of an offence under this Section as a result of his wife's inability to consent, provided he genuinely believes her to be his wife and has reasonable grounds for such a belief (Section 14(3) Sexual Offences Act 1956).

The provisions for the anonymity of alleged victims to this offence are contained within Section 1 Sexual Offences (Amendment) Act 1992.

Punishable

on indictment with 10 years' imprisonment.

3.17. Indecent assault on a man

> It is an offence for a person to make an indecent assault on a man.
>
> Section 15 Sexual Offences Act 1956

Notes

'Indecent assault' has the same meaning as for an Indecent Assault on a Woman (see 3.16).

'Man' includes **'boy'** (Section 46 Sexual Offences Act 1956).

A boy under 16 years of age cannot give consent to an assault under this Section (Section 15(2) Sexual Offences Act 1956).

The provisions for the anonymity of alleged victims to this offence are contained within Section 1 Sexual Offences (Amendment) Act 1992.

Punishable

on indictment with 10 years' imprisonment.

3.18. Indecency with or towards a child

> It is an offence for a person to commit an Act of gross indecency with or towards a child under 16 years of age - or to incite a child under that age to such an act - with her or him or another.
>
> Section 1 Indecency with Children Act 1960 as amended by Section 39 Criminal Justice and Court Services Act 2000

Notes

Whether an act amounts to one of **'gross indecency'** is for the jury to decide.

This Act was primarily passed to cater for circumstances that fell short of an indecent assault because the defendant did not actually touch the child but rather confined his activities to encouraging the child to touch him without making the kind of threats constituent of an assault.

The Act is, however, by no means limited to these circumstances. For example, in *R v Speck* 1977 (2 All ER 859) it was held that passive inactivity on the part of the defendant in response to an eight-year-old girl putting her hand on his penis for about five minutes amounted to an invitation towards the child to continue her behaviour.

In addition, in *R v Francis* 1988 (88 Cr App Rep 127) it was held that a man had committed this offence in circumstances in which he was masturbating in front of children and deriving satisfaction from the knowledge that they were watching him, even though he had done nothing more to deliberately attract their attention.

The provisions for the anonymity of alleged victims to this offence are contained within Section 1 Sexual Offences (Amendment) Act 1992.

Example

A charge under this Section may be considered when an act of gross indecency has taken place in the absence of circumstances amounting to an indecent assault. A person who masturbates in front of a child or encourages a child to perform a sexual act on her or him - but does not physically touch or threaten the child - might be guilty of this offence.

Punishable

on indictment with 10 years' imprisonment (as amended by Section 52 Crime (Sentences) Act 1997).

3.19. Indecent exposure

> It is an offence for any person to wilfully, openly, lewdly and obscenely, to expose his person with intent to insult any person.
>
> Section 4 Vagrancy Act 1824

Notes

'Person' means penis (*Evans v Ewels* 1972 (2All ER 22)).

This offence can be committed in a private place (*Ford V Falcone* 1971 (2 All ER 1138)).

Punishable

on a summary basis only with three months' imprisonment.

3.20. Abduction of a woman by force or for the sake of her property with the intention of marriage or unlawful sexual intercourse

> It is an offence for a person to take away or detain a woman against her will - with the intention that she shall marry or have unlawful sexual intercourse with that or any other person - if she is so taken away or detained either by force or for the sake of her property or expectations of property.
>
> Section 17 Sexual Offences Act 1956

Notes

'Woman' includes **'girl'** (Section 46 Sexual Offences Act 1956).

'Unlawful' has the same meaning as in Administering Drugs to Obtain or Facilitate Intercourse (see 3.4).

'Sexual intercourse' has the same meaning as in Rape (see 3.1).

'Property' includes any interest in property - **'expectations of property'** relate only to a person who is the woman's next of kin or one of the next of kin (S 17(2) Sexual Offences Act 1956).

Punishable

on indictment with 14 years' imprisonment.

3.21. Abduction of an unmarried girl under 18 from her parent or guardian for the purposes of unlawful sexual intercourse

> It is an offence, subject to the exception mentioned below - for a person to take an unmarried girl under the age of 18 years from the possession of her parent or guardian against her or his will - if she is so taken with the intention that she shall have unlawful sexual intercourse with men or a particular man.
>
> Section 19 Sexual Offences Act 1956

Notes

A person is not guilty of an offence under this Section if - in taking a girl under these circumstances - she or he believes the girl to be over the age of 18 years and has reasonable cause for the belief (Section 19(2) Sexual Offences Act 1956).

'Unlawful' has the same meaning as in Administering Drugs to Obtain or Facilitate Intercourse (see 3.4).

'Sexual intercourse' has the same meaning as in Rape (see 3.1).

'Guardian' means any person having parental responsibility for or care of the girl. **'Parental**

FIG 4: OFFENCES OF INDECENCY

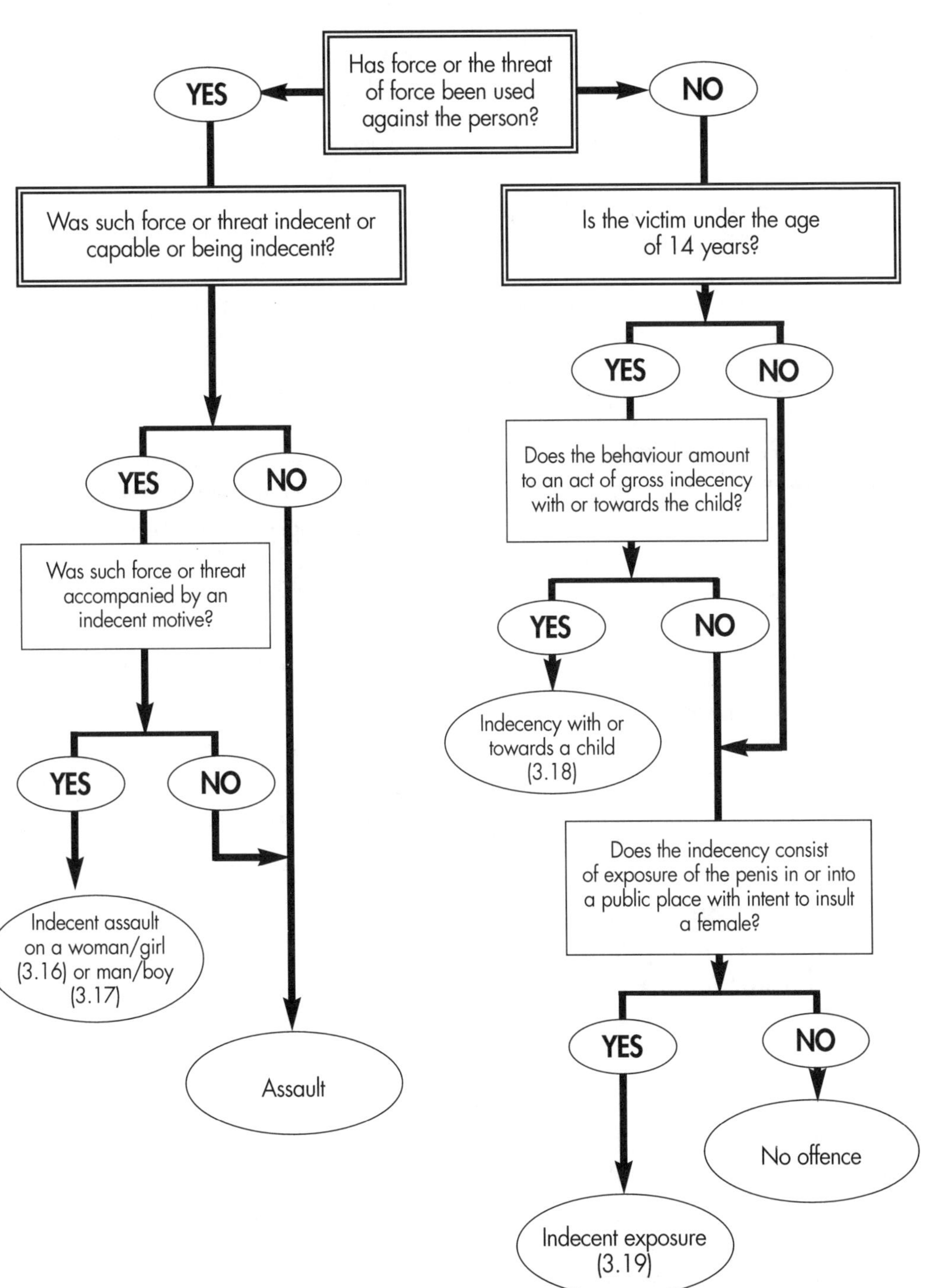

'responsibility' - same meaning as in the Children Act 1989 (see Notes to Chapter 1, Police Protection).

'Right to marry' - there is a right under ECHR Article 12 for every person of a marriageable age to marry (see Chapter 10).

Punishable

on indictment with two years' imprisonment.

3.22. Abduction of unmarried girl under 16 from parent or guardian

> It is an offence for a person - acting without lawful authority or excuse - to take an unmarried girl under the age of 16 years from the possession of her parent or guardian against her or his will.
>
> Section 20 Sexual Offences Act 1956

Notes

It is not necessary to prove any particular intention to support a charge under this Section, but there must be evidence of an intent to abduct the child.

'Guardian' means any person having parental responsibility for or care of the girl.

'Parental responsibility' has the same meaning as in the Children Act 1989 (see the Notes to Chapter 1, Police Protection).

Punishable

on indictment with two years' imprisonment.

3.23. Abduction of a defective from her parent or guardian for unlawful sexual intercourse

> It is an offence - subject to the exception mentioned below - for a person to take a woman who is a defective from the possession of her parent or guardian against her or his will - if she is so taken with the intention that she shall have unlawful sexual intercourse with men or a particular man.
>
> Section 21 Sexual Offences Act 1956

Notes

A person is not guilty of an offence under this Section if - in taking a woman under these circumstances - she or he does not know and has no reason to suspect that the woman is a defective (Section 21(2) Sexual Offences Act 1956).

'Woman' includes **'girl'** (Section 46 Sexual Offences Act 1956).

The unfortunate, offensive and rather dated term **'defective'** has the same meaning as outlined in Intercourse with a Defective (see 3.8).

'Unlawful' has the same meaning as in Administering Drugs to Obtain or Facilitate Intercourse (see 3.4).

'Sexual intercourse' has the same meaning as in Rape (see 3.1).

'Guardian' means any person having parental responsibility for or care of the girl or woman.

'Parental responsibility' has the same meaning as in the Children Act 1989, as shown in the Notes to Chapter 1, Police Protection.

Punishable

on indictment with two years' imprisonment.

3.24. Causing or encouraging the prostitution of, intercourse with or indecent assault on girl under 16

> It is an offence for a person to cause or encourage the prostitution of - or the commission of unlawful sexual intercourse with - or an indecent assault on - a girl under the age of 16 years - for whom that person is responsible.
>
> S 28(1) Sexual Offences Act 1956

Notes

In cases in which a girl has become a prostitute, has had unlawful sexual intercourse, or has been indecently assaulted - a person will be deemed to have committed this offence if she or he knowingly allowed the girl to consort with, or enter or continue in the employment of, any prostitute or person of known immoral character (Section 28(2) Sexual Offences Act 1956).

'Unlawful' has the same meaning as in Administering Drugs to Obtain or Facilitate Intercourse (see 3.4).

'Sexual intercourse' has the same meaning as in Rape (see 3.1).

'Indecent assault' has the same meaning as in Indecent Assault on a Woman (see 3.16).

Persons who are treated as being **'responsible'** for a girl (for the purposes of this Section) are:

a. her parents;
b. any person who is not a parent of hers but who has parental responsibility for her; and
c. any person who has care of her.

A person falling into categories a. and b. above will not be regarded as being responsible for the girl if either a care order or a residence order* - in which that person is not named - is in force in respect of her (Section 28(3) and (4) Sexual Offences Act 1956).

* see Chapter 2, Protection Orders

Example

This offence might be committed by a parent or guardian who encourages a child in her or his care to have unlawful sexual intercourse.

Punishable

on indictment with two years' imprisonment.

3.25. Permitting girl under 13 to use premises for intercourse

> It is an offence for a person - who is the owner or occupier of any premises, or who has or assists in the management or control of any premises - to induce or knowingly suffer a girl under the age of 13 years to resort to or to be on the premises - for the purpose of having unlawful sexual intercourse with men or with a particular man.
>
> Section 25 Sexual Offences Act, 1956

Notes

'Unlawful' has the same meaning as in Administering Drugs to Obtain or Facilitate Intercourse (see 3.4).

'Sexual intercourse' has the same meaning as in Rape (see 3.1).

Example

This offence might be committed if the occupier of premises allows her or his premises to be used by girls of 12 years of age and under, for the purposes of unlawful sexual intercourse.

Punishable

on indictment with life imprisonment.

3.26. Permitting a girl under 16 to use premises for intercourse

> It is an offence for a person - who is the owner or occupier of any premises, or who has or assists in the management or control of any premises - to induce or knowingly suffer a girl under the age of 16 years to resort to or to be on the premises - for the purpose of having unlawful sexual intercourse with men or with a particular man.
>
> Section 26 Sexual Offences Act 1956

Note

'Unlawful' has the same meaning as in Administering Drugs to Obtain or Facilitate Intercourse (see 3.4).

'Sexual intercourse' has the same meaning as in Rape (see 3.1).

Example

This offence might be committed if the occupier of premises allows her or his premises to be used by girls of 15 years of age and under, for the purposes of unlawful sexual intercourse.

Punishable

on indictment with two years' imprisonment.

3.27. Permitting a defective to use premises for purpose of unlawful sexual intercourse

> It is an offence - subject to the exception below - for a person who is the owner or occupier of any premises, or who has or assists in the management or control of any premises - to induce or knowingly suffer a woman who is a defective - to resort to or to be on the premises for the purpose of having unlawful sexual intercourse with men or with a particular man.
>
> Section 27 Sexual Offences Act 1956

Notes

A person is not guilty of an offence under this Section if she or he does not know and has no reason to suspect that the woman is a defective (Section 27(2) Sexual Offences Act 1956).

'Woman' includes **'girl'** (Section 46 Sexual Offences Act 1956).

The unfortunate offensive and rather dated term **'defective'** has the same meaning outlined in Intercourse with a Defective (see 3.8).

'Unlawful' has the same meaning as in Administering Drugs to Obtain or Facilitate Intercourse (see 3.4).

'Sexual intercourse' has the same meaning as in Rape (see 3.1).

Punishable

on indictment with two years' imprisonment.

3.28. Taking, distributing or showing indecent photographs or pseudo-photographs of children

> It is an offence to:
>
> (a) take or permit to be taken, or to make, any indecent photograph or pseudo-photograph of a child; or
>
> (b) distribute or show any indecent photographs or pseudo-photographs of a child; or
>
> (c) possess any indecent photographs or pseudo-photographs of a child with a view to their being distributed or shown by her or himself or others; or
>
> (d) publish or cause to be published any advertisement likely to be understood as conveying the impression that the advertiser distributes or shows indecent photographs or pseudo-photographs of a child, or intends to do so.
>
> Section 1(1) Protection of Children Act 1978 as amended by the Criminal Justice and Public Order Act 1994

Notes

'Indecent' is not defined but will be a matter for the court.

'Indecent photograph' includes films, and copies of photographs and films, and any indecent photograph included within a film. It also includes negatives, data stored on computer disc or by other electronic means capable of converting it into a photograph, and any form of video recording (Section 7(2) and (4) Protection of Children Act 1978).

'Pseudo-photograph' means an image, whether made by computer graphics or otherwise, which appears to be a photograph. It also includes a copy of an indecent pseudo-photograph and data stored on computer disc or by other electronic means capable of converting it into a pseudo-photograph (S 7(7) and (9) Protection of Children Act 1978).

'Child' means a person under 16 years of age (Section 7(6) Protection of Children Act 1978).

If the impression conveyed by a pseudo-photograph is that the person shown is a child, the pseudo-photograph shall be treated for the purposes of this Act as showing a child - as shall a pseudo-photograph in which the predominant impression conveyed is that the person shown is a child, notwithstanding that some of the physical characteristics shown are those of an adult (Section 7(8) Protection of Children Act 1978).

'Distribute' means parting with possession of the indecent photographs or pseudo-photographs, or exposing or offering them for acquisition by another person (Section 1(2) Protection of Children Act 1978).

If a person is charged with distributing, showing or possessing the indecent photographs or pseudo-photographs with a view to their being distributed or shown, it will be a defence for her or him to prove that she or he had a legitimate reason for having them in her or his possession. In these circumstances it will also be a defence for the accused to prove that she or he had not seen the photographs or pseudo-photographs and did not know nor had any cause to suspect them to be indecent (Section 1(4) Protection of Children Act 1978).

Search warrants for such material may be obtained under Section 4 Protection of Children Act 1978.

Example

This offence could be considered in most cases in which a person is in possession of the photographs for reasons other than purely her or his own personal use. In circumstances when the photographs are in the possession of a person solely for their own use, a charge may be considered under Section 160 of the Criminal Justice Act 1988 (as follows).

Punishable

on indictment with 10 years' imprisonment (Section 6 Protection of Children Act 1978 as amended by Section 41 Criminal Justice and Court Services Act 2000.

3.29. Possessing indecent photographs or pseudo-photographs of children

> It is an offence to possess an indecent photograph or pseudo-photograph of a child.
>
> Section 160(1) Criminal Justice Act 1988 as amended by the Criminal Justice and Public Order Act 1994

Notes

'Indecent', **'indecent photograph'**, **'pseudo-photograph'** and **'child'** have the same meanings as for Taking, Distributing or Showing Indecent Photographs or Pseudo-Photographs of Children (previous page).

If a person is charged with possessing indecent photographs or pseudo-photographs under this Section, it will be a defence for her or him to prove:

a. that she or he had a legitimate reason for having them in her or his possession; or
b. that she or he had not seen the photographs or pseudo-photographs and did not know nor had any cause to suspect them to be indecent; or
c. that the photograph was sent to the accused without her or him asking for it and she or he did not keep it for an unreasonable length of time;

(Section 160(2) Criminal Justice Act 1988).

Example

The charging of this offence may be considered if a person is found to be in possession of these photographs purely for his or her own personal use.

Punishable

on indictment with five years' imprisonment (Section 160 Criminal Justice Act 1988 as amended by Section 41 Criminal Justice and Court Services Act 2000).

3.30. Printing, publishing, selling, hiring etc, harmful publications to children and young people

Any person - who prints, publishes, sells or lets on hire - or has in her or his possession for the purpose of selling or letting on hire - any book, magazine or like work which is of a kind likely to fall into the hands of children or young persons - and which consists wholly or mainly of stories told in pictures (with or without the addition of written material) and portraying:

a. the commission of crimes; or

b. acts of violence or cruelty; or

c. incidents of a repulsive or horrible nature;

in such a way that the work as a whole would tend to corrupt a child or young person into whose hands it might fall - shall be guilty of an offence.

Sections 1 and 2 Children and Young Persons (Harmful Publications) Act 1955

Notes

'Child' means a person under the age of 14 years.

'Young person' means a person who has attained the age of 14 years but is under the age of 18 years (Section 5(2) Children and Young Persons (Harmful Publications) Act 1955).

Search warrants for this material may be obtained under Section 3 Children and Young Persons (Harmful Publications) Act 1955.

Example

A charge under this Section might be considered if a person is found to be in possession of a comic or a picture book of an indecent nature which she or he intends to sell to a child or young person. The possession here would need to be with a view to selling or hiring. Unless responsible for printing or publishing it, possession of this material with intent to simply give it to a child would not constitute an offence under this Section

Punishable

on a summary basis only with four months' imprisonment.

3.31. Sending a malicious communication

Any person who sends to another person:

a. a letter or other article which conveys -
   i. a message which is indecent or grossly offensive,
   ii. a threat, or
   iii. information which is false and known or believed to be false by the sender; or

b. any other article which is, in whole or in part, of an indecent or grossly offensive nature;

is guilty of an offence - if her or his purpose or one of her or his purposes in sending it - is that it should (so far as Paragraphs (a) and (b) above are concerned) cause distress or anxiety to the recipient - or to any other person to whom she or he intends that its contents or nature should be communicated.

Section 1(1) Malicious Communications Act 1988

Notes

'Sending' includes delivering and causing to be sent or delivered and **'sender'** is to be construed accordingly (Section 1(3) Malicious Communications Act 1988).

A person is not guilty of an offence by virtue of Section 1(a)(ii) above if she or he shows:

a. that the threat was used to reinforce a demand which she or he believed she or he had reasonable grounds for making; and
b. that she or he believed that the use of the threat was a proper means of reinforcing the demand;

(Section 1(2) Malicious Communications Act 1988).

Example

The sending of an indecent message to a child - with the intention that it should cause some distress, either to the child or her or his caregivers - might amount to an offence under this Section.

Punishable

on a summary basis only with a level 4 fine (- £2,500 at the time of going to press).

3.32. Abuse of position of trust

> It is an offence for a person aged 18 or over to have sexual intercourse (whether vaginal or anal) with a person under that age or to engage in any other sexual activity with or directed towards such a person if he or she is in a position of trust in relation to that person.
>
> Section 3(1) Sexual Offences (Amendment) Act 2000

Notes

Where a person is charged with this offence, it is a defence to prove that, at the time of the intercourse or other sexual activity:

a. he or she did not know, and could not reasonably have been expected to know, that the other person was under 18 years of age;
b. he or she did not know, and could not reasonably have been expected to know, that he or she was in a position of trust in relation to the other person; or
c. he or she was lawfully married to the other person;

(Section 3(2) Sexual Offences (Amendment) Act 2000).

In addition, it is not an offence under this Section if - immediately before the commencement of this Act (January 8,.2001) - a person aged 18 or over was in a position of trust in relation to a person under that age and a sexual relationship already existed between them (Section 3(3) Sexual Offences (Amendment) Act 2000).

'Sexual activity' means any activity which a reasonable person would regard as sexual in all the circumstances, but does not include something that rests solely on the intentions, motives or feelings of the parties. This suggests that intentions and feelings are not sufficient in themselves, there must be an act that could be regarded as sexual in addition to this (Section 3(5) Sexual Offences (Amendment) Act 2000).

'Position of trust' - A person aged 18 or over can be regarded as being in a 'position of trust' in relation to a person under that age if:

a. he or she **'looks after'** people under 18 who are detained in an institution by virtue of an order of a court or under an enactment and the person under that age is detained in that institution;
b. he or she **'looks after'** persons under 18 who are resident in a home or other place provided by a local authority or voluntary organisation and the person under that age is provided with accommodation and maintenance or accommodation in that place.
c. he or she **'looks after'** persons under 18 who are accommodated and cared for in an institution which is a hospital, a residential care home, nursing home, mental nursing home, private hospital, community home, voluntary home, children's home, residential establishment; or a home provided by the government under Section 82(5) of the Children Act 1989 and the person under that age is accommodated and cared for in that institution.
d. he or she **'looks after'** persons under 18 who are receiving full-time education at an educational institution and the person under that age is receiving education in that institution.

A person **'looks after'** persons under 18 for the purposes of this section if he is regularly involved in caring for, training, supervising or being in sole charge of such persons (Section 4 Sexual Offences [Amendment] Act 2000).

Punishable

on indictment with five years' imprisonment for a term not exceeding five years.

3.33. Sexual offences committed outside the UK

3.33a..Extension of jurisdiction to certain sexual offences committed outside the United Kingdom

Section 7 and Schedule 2, Sex Offenders Act 1997

Ss (1)

Subject to Sub-section (2) below, any act done by a person in a country or territory outside the United Kingdom which:

(a) constituted an offence under the law in force in that country or territory; and

(b) would constitute a sexual offence to which this Section applies had it been done in England and Wales or in Northern Ireland;

shall constitute that sexual offence under the law of that part of the United Kingdom.

Ss (2)

No proceedings shall be brought against any person by virtue of this Section - unless she or he was a British Citizen or resident in the United Kingdom on the date of the commencement of this Section (1.9.97) - or has subsequently become a British Citizen or resident in the United Kingdom.

Ss (3)

An act punishable under the law in any country or territory constitutes an offence under that law for the purposes of this Section, however it is described in that law.

Ss (4)

Subject to Sub-section (5), the condition in Sub-section (1)(a) shall be taken to be satisfied unless - not later than the rules of court may provide - the defence serves on the prosecution a notice:

(a) stating that, on the facts as alleged with respect to the act in question, the condition is not in its opinion satisfied;

(b) showing the grounds for that opinion; and

(c) requiring the prosecution to show that the condition is satisfied.

Ss (5)

The court, if it thinks fit, may permit the defence to require the prosecution to show that the condition is satisfied without prior service of a notice under Sub-section (4).

Ss (6)

In the Crown court, the question of whether the condition is satisfied is to be decided by the judge alone.

Ss (7)

The offences to which this Section applies are:

- Rape (Section 1 Sexual Offences Act 1956) - if the victim was under 16 years of age at the time of the alleged offence;
- Unlawful Sexual Intercourse With a Girl Under 13 Years (Section 5 Sexual Offences Act 1956);
- Unlawful Sexual Intercourse With a Girl Under 16 Years (Section 6 Sexual Offences Act 1956);
- Buggery - if the victim was under 16 years of age at the time of the alleged offence (Section 12 Sexual Offences Act 1956);
- Indecent Assault on a Girl - if the victim was under 16 years of age at the time of the alleged offence (Section 14 Sexual Offences Act 1956);
- Indecent Assault on a Boy - if the victim was under 16 years of age at the time of the alleged offence (Section 15 Sexual Offences Act 1956);
- Assault With Intent to Commit Buggery - if the victim was under 16 years of age at the time of the alleged offence (Section 16 Sexual Offences Act 1956);
- Indecency With or Towards a Child (Section 1 Indecency with Children Act 1960); and
- Taking, Distributing or Showing etc Indecent Photographs of Children (Section 1 Protection of Children Act 1978).

Note

This Act (Sex Offenders Act 1997) commenced on September 1, 1997

3.33b.Conspiracy and incitement to commit certain sexual offences outside the United Kingdom

Sections 1 - 3 Sexual Offences (Conspiracy and Incitement) Act 1996

Section 1

Ss (1)

If each of the following conditions is satisfied in the case of any **'agreement'**, Part I of the Criminal Law Act 1977 (conspiracy) has effect in relation to the agreement as it has effect in relation to an agreement falling within its own Section 1(1).

Ss (2)

The first condition is that the pursuit of the agreed course of conduct would at some stage involve:

(a) an act by one or more of the parties; or

(b) the happening of some other event;

intended to take place in a country or territory outside the United Kingdom.

Ss (3)

The second condition is that that act or other event constitutes an offence under the law in force in that country or territory.

Ss (4)

The third condition is that the agreement would fall within Section 1(1) of the Criminal Law Act 1977 as an agreement relating to the commission of a **'listed sexual offence'** but for the fact that the offence would take place outside the UK - **'would not be an offence triable in England and Wales'** - if committed in accordance with the parties' intentions.

Ss (5)

The forth condition is that:

(a) a party to the agreement, or a party's agent, did anything in England and Wales in relation to the agreement before its formation; or

(b) a party to the agreement became a party in England and Wales (by joining it either in person or through an agent); or

(c) a party to the agreement, or a party's agent, did or omitted anything in England and Wales in pursuance of the agreement.

Ss (6)

In the application of Part I of the Criminal Law Act 1977 to such an agreement, any reference to an offence is to be read as a reference to what would be the listed sexual offence in question, but for the fact that it is not an offence triable in England and Wales.

Notes

When the term **'agreement'** is used in this Act, it has the same meaning as when it is used in Part I of the Criminal Law Act 1977 in relation to the offence of conspiracy. In these circumstances, a person is guilty of conspiracy if she or he enters into an agreement with any other person or persons to pursue a course of conduct which would amount to or involve the commission of any offence(s) by one or more parties to the agreement - or would amount to or involve the commission of any offence(s) by one or more parties to the agreement but for the existence of facts which make the commission of the offence(s) impossible.

'Listed sexual offence' includes:

- Rape (Section 1 Sexual Offences Act 1956) - if the victim was under 16 years of age at the time of the alleged offence;
- Unlawful Sexual Intercourse With a Girl Under 13 Years (Section 5 Sexual Offences Act 1956);
- Unlawful Sexual Intercourse With a Girl under 16 Years (S 6 Sexual Offences Act 1956);
- Buggery - if the victim was under 16 years of age at the time of the alleged offence (Section 12 Sexual Offences Act 1956);
- Indecent Assault on a Girl - if the victim was under 16 years at the time of the alleged offence (S 14 Sexual Offences Act 1956);
- Indecent Assault on a Boy - if the victim was under 16 years at the time of the alleged offence (S 15 Sexual Offences Act 1956);
- Indecency With or Towards a Child (Section 1 Indecency with Children Act 1960);

(Schedule to Sexual Offences (Conspiracy and Incitement) Act 1996).

'Would not be an offence triable in England and Wales' ie would not fall within the jurisdiction of the English or Welsh courts. Sub-section (4) therefore means that the circumstances must be such - that an offence of conspiracy under Section 1 Criminal Law Act 1977 in respect of a listed sexual offence - could have been preferred against the accused - had what they had in view fallen within the jurisdiction of the English or Welsh courts.

Section 2

Ss (1)

This Section applies if:

(a) any act done by a person in England and Wales would amount to the offence of incitement to commit a listed sexual offence but for the fact that what she or he had in view would not be an offence triable in England and Wales;

(b) the whole or part of what she or he had in view was intended to take place in a country or territory outside the United Kingdom; and

(c) what she or he had in view would involve the commission of an offence under the law in force in that country or territory.

Ss (2)

In cases in which this Section applies:

(a) what she or he had in view is to be treated as that listed sexual offence for the purposes of any charge of incitement brought in respect of that act; and

(b) any such charge is accordingly triable in England and Wales.

Ss (3)

Any act of incitement by means of a message (however communicated) is to be treated as done in England and Wales if the message is sent or received in England and Wales.

Section 3

Ss (1)

Conduct punishable under the law in force in any country or territory is an offence under that law for the purposes of Sections (1) and (2), however it is described in that law.

Ss (2)

Subject to Sub-section (3), a condition in Section 1(3) or 2(1)(c) is to be taken as satisfied unless, not later than rules of court may provide, the defence serves on the prosecution a notice:

(a) stating that, on the facts as alleged with respect to the relevant conduct (see Sub-section (3) below), the condition is not in their opinion satisfied;

(b) showing the grounds for that opinion; and

(c) requiring the prosecution to show it is satisfied.

Ss (3)

In Sub-section (2) the **'relevant conduct'** means:

(a) when a condition in Section 1(3) is in question, the agreed course of conduct; and

(b) when the condition in Section 2(1)(c) is in question - what the accused had in view.

Ss (4)

The court, if it thinks fit, may permit the defence to require the prosecution to show that the condition is satisfied without prior service of a notice under Sub-section (2).

Ss (5)

In the Crown court, the question of whether the condition is satisfied is to be decided by the judge alone.

Ss (6)

In any proceedings in respect of any offence triable by virtue of Sections 1 or 2, it is immaterial to guilt whether or not the accused was a British Citizen at the time of - any act or other event of which proof is required - for conviction of the offence.

Ss (7)

References to an offence of conspiracy to commit a listed sexual offence include an offence triable in England and Wales as such a conspiracy by virtue of Section 1 (without prejudice to Sub-section (6) of that Section).

(See Sub-section 9 below for further explanation of this Sub-section.)

Ss (8)

References to an offence of incitement to commit a listed sexual offence include an offence triable in England and Wales as such an incitement by virtue of Section 2 (without prejudice to Sub-section (2) of that Section).

(See Sub-section (9) below for further explanation of this Sub-section.)

Ss (9)

Sub-sections (7) and (8) apply to references in any enactment, instrument or document (except those listed in Sections 1 and 2 of this Act and in Part I Criminal Law Act 1977).*

* This means that this Act applies in cases in which any other Act, Statutory Instrument or Document refers either to a conspiracy or an incitement to commit a listed sexual offence.

3.34. Notification requirements for persons convicted of sexual offences

Sections 1-3 (Part I) Sex Offenders Act 1997

Section 1

Ss (1)

A person becomes subject to the notification requirements described under Sections 1 to 3 of this Act if, on or after 1.9.97 (the commencement date of this Part of the Act):

(a) she or he is **'convicted'** of a sexual offence to which this Part of the Act applies;

(b) she or he is **'found guilty'** of such an offence by reason of insanity, or to be under a **'disability'** and to have done the act she or he was charged with in respect of such an offence;

(c) she or he is cautioned by a constable in England and Wales or Northern Ireland in respect of such an offence which she or he admitted at the time the caution was given.

Ss (2)

A person becomes subject to those requirements if, at that commencement (on or after 1.9.97):

(a) she or he has been convicted of a sexual offence to which this Part of the Act applies but has not been dealt with in respect of that offence;

(b) she or he has been found guilty of such an offence by reason of insanity, or to be under a disability and to have done the act she or he was charged with in respect of such an offence, but has not been dealt with in respect of the finding.

Ss (3)

A person becomes subject to those requirements if, at that commencement (on or after 1.9.97):

(a) she or he is serving a sentence of imprisonment or a term of service detention or is subject to a community order in respect of a sexual offence to which this Part of the Act applies;

(b) she or he is subject to **'supervision'**, having been released from prison after serving the whole or part of a sentence of imprisonment in respect of such an offence;

(c) she or he is detained in a hospital or is subject to a guardianship order having been convicted of such an offence; or

(d) she or he is detained in a hospital having been found not guilty of such an offence by reason of insanity - or to be under a disability and to have done the act she or he was charged with in respect of such an offence;

and a person who would fall within Paragraphs (a), (c) or (d) above - but for the fact that at that commencement (on or after September 1, 1997) she or he is unlawfully at large or absent without leave, on temporary release or leave of absence, or on bail pending an appeal - shall be treated as falling within that Paragraph.

Ss (4)

A person falling within Sub-sections (1) to (3) above shall continue to be subject to those requirements for a period of time as follows:

A person:

- who is or has been sentenced to imprisonment for life, or for a term of 30 months or more, in respect of the offence - *an indefinite period;*
- who is or has been admitted to a hospital and is subject to a restriction order in respect of the offence or finding - *an indefinite period;*

- who is or has been sentenced to imprisonment for a term of more than six months but less than 30 months in respect of the offence - *a period of 10 years beginning with the* **'relevant date'**;
- who is or has been sentenced to imprisonment for a term of six months or less in respect of the offence - *a period of seven years beginning with the relevant date;*
- who is or has been admitted to a hospital without being subject to a restriction order in respect of the offence or finding - *a period of seven years beginning with the relevant date;*
- of any other description (including those convicted of the offences to which this Part of the Act applies but not sentenced to a term of imprisonment and to those who are cautioned having admitted the offence etc) - *a period of five years beginning with the relevant date.*

Ss (5)

Sub-section (6) below applies when a person falling within Sub-sections (1)(a), 2(a) or (3)(a), (b) or (c) above is or has been sentenced - in respect of two or more sexual offences to which this Part of the Act applies:

(a) to consecutive terms of imprisonment;

(b) to terms of imprisonment which are partly concurrent.

Ss (6)

Sub-section (4) above shall have effect as if the person were or had been sentenced in respect of each of the offences, to a term of imprisonment which:

(a) in the case of consecutive terms, is equal to the total of those terms when added together;

(b) in the case of concurrent terms, is equal to the total of those terms when added together after making such a deduction as may be necessary to ensure that no period of time is counted more than once.

Ss (7)

If a person - found to be under a disability and to have done the act she or he was charged with in respect of a sexual offence to which this Part of the Act applies - is subsequently tried for the offence, the finding and any order made in respect of the finding shall be disregarded for the purposes of this Section. *

* This Sub-section refers to circumstances in which an accused person is considered fit to be tried after having previously been considered unfit to be tried by virtue of mental or physical disability. In these circumstances, the original finding that the accused did the act she or he was charged with doing is set aside and a new trial begins.

Ss (8)

In this Part of the Act, the **'relevant date'** means:

(a) in the case of a person falling within Sub-sections (1)(a), (2)(a) or (3)(a), (b) or (c) above, the date of conviction;

(b) in the case of a person falling within Sub-sections (1)(b), (2)(b) or (3)(d) above, the date of the finding;

(c) in the case of a person falling within Sub-sections (1)(c) above - the date of the caution.

Notes

A **'conviction'** means convicted of the offence before a court having the jurisdiction to hear the case and while being fit to be tried.

Being **'found guilty'** of an offence means that a court having jurisdiction to hear the case considers the accused to have committed the act comprising the offence in circumstances in which she or he is unfit to be tried by insanity or disability.

'Disability' includes mental or physical disability – though instances in which a person is unfit to be tried by reason of physical disability are rare in modern times. However these would include, for example, circumstances in which an accused person could not speak or hear and was unable to read or communicate by any other means.

'Supervision' - A person who has been released from prison on licence or parole is subject to supervision by the Probation Service.

'Private life' - Where the police circulate information about prolific offenders (for example paedophiles) and place it in the public domain, there is an infringement of the alleged criminals' rights (ECHR Article 8). A fair balance must be struck between the general interests of the community and the interests of individuals. Clear protocols exist for exchange of information on convicted paedophiles and the require-ment for registration of domicile with local police.

Section 2

as amended by Schedule 5 of the Criminal Justice and Court Services Act, 2000

Ss (1)

A person who is subject to the notification requirements of this Part of the Act shall, before the end of the period of three days beginning with the relevant date, notify the following information to the police:

(a) her or his name and - if she or he also uses one or more other names - each of those names;

(b) her or his home address.

Ss (2)

A person who is subject to those requirements shall also - before the end of a three-day period beginning with the following new circumstances:

(a) her or his use of a name that has not been notified to the police under this Section;

(b) any change of her or his home address;

(c) her or his having resided or stayed, for a qualifying period, at any premises in the United Kingdom the address of which has not been notified to the police under this Section;

notify that name, the effect of that change or, as the case may be, the address of those premises, to the police.

Ss (3)

Notification given to the police by any person shall not be regarded as complying with Sub-sections (1) or (2) above unless it also states:

(a) her or his date of birth;

(b) her or his name on the relevant date and - if she or he used one or more other names on that date - each of those names;

(c) her or his home address on that date.

Ss (4)

For the purposes of determining any three-day period for the purposes of Sub-sections (1) or (2) above, there shall be disregarded any period of time during which the person in question:

(a) is remanded in or committed to custody by an order of a court;

(b) is serving a sentence of imprisonment or a term of service detention;

(c) is detained in a hospital; or

(d) is outside the United Kingdom.

Ss (5)

A person may give notice under this Section:

(a) by attending any police station in her/his local police area and giving an oral notification to any police officer or to any person authorised for the purpose by the officer in charge of the station;

(b) by sending a written notification to any such police station.

Ss (6)

Any notification under this Section shall be acknowledged. Acknowledgements under this Sub-section shall be in writing and in such form as the Secretary of State may direct.

Ss (7)

In this Section:

'Home address' in relation to any person means the address of her or his home - that is to say her or his sole or main residence in the United Kingdom or - if she or he has no such residence - premises in the UK she or he regularly visits.

'Local police area' in relation to any person means the police area in which her or his home is situated.

'Qualifying period' means:

(a) a period of three days; or

(b) two or more periods in any period of 12 months which, taken together, amount to three days.

Section 3

Ss (1)

If a person:

(a) fails, without reasonable excuse, to comply with Section 2(1) or (2) (previous page); or

(b) notifies to the police in purported compliance with Section 2(1) or (2), any information which she or he knows to be false;

she or he will be liable on summary conviction to a term of imprisonment not exceeding six months.

Ss (2)

A person commits an offence under Sub-section (1)(a) above on the day on which she or he first fails, without reasonable excuse, to comply with Section 2(1) or (2) - and continues to commit it throughout any period during which the failure continues. However a person shall not be prosecuted under that provision more than once in respect of the same failure.

Notes

The date of **'commencement'** for Sections 1 to 3 (Part I) of the Sex Offenders Act 1997 was 1.9.97.

This Part of the Act applies to the following offences:

- Rape (Section 1 Sexual Offences Act 1956);
- Unlawful Sexual Intercourse With a Girl Under 13 Years (Section 5 Sexual Offences Act 1956);
- Unlawful Sexual Intercourse With a Girl Under 16 Years - if the offender is 20 years or over (Section 6 Sexual Offences Act 1956);
- Incest by a Man - if the victim or other party to the offence is under 18 years of age (Section 10 Sexual Offences Act 1956);
- Buggery - if the offender is 20 years or over and the victim or other party to the offence is under 18 years (S 12 Sexual Offences Act 1956);
- Indecency Between Men - if the offender is 20 years or over and the victim or other party to the offence is under 18 years of age (Section 13 Sexual Offences Act 1956);
- Indecent Assault on a Woman - if the victim to the offence was under 18 years of age - and in any case in which the offender is or was either sentenced to a term of imprisonment or 30 months or more, or admitted to a hospital subject to a restriction order (S 14 Sexual Offences Act 1956);
- Indecent Assault on a Man - if the victim to the offence was under 18 years of age - and in any case in which the offender is or was either sentenced to a term of imprisonment or 30 months or more, or admitted to a hospital subject to a restriction order (S 15 Sexual Offences Act 1956);
- Assault with Intent to Commit Buggery - if the victim to the offence is under 18 years of age (Section 16 Sexual Offences Act 1956);
- Causing or Encouraging the Prostitution of, Indecent Assault on, or Intercourse With, a Girl Under 16 Years (S 28 Sexual Offences Act 1956);
- Indecency With or Towards a Child (Section 1 Indecency with Children Act 1960);
- Inciting a girl under 16 years of age to have incest (Section 54 Criminal Law Act 1977);
- Taking, Distributing or Showing etc Indecent Photographs of Children (Section 1 Protection of Children Act 1978);
- Possession of Indecent Photographs of Children (Section 160 Criminal Justice Act 1988);
- Importing Prohibited Goods in the Form of Indecent Photographs of Children Under 16 Years (S 170 Customs and Excise Management Act 1979).
- Abuse of a Position of Trust (Section 3 Sexual Offences (Amendment) Act 2000).

3.35. Sex Offender Orders

Sections 2 to 4 Crime and Disorder Act 1998

Section 2

Ss (1)

If it appears to a chief officer of police that the following conditions are fulfilled with respect to any person in her or his police area:

(a) that the person is a **'sex offender'** (S 3(1)); and

(b) that the person has acted, since the **'relevant date'** (see Section 3(2) following page), in such a way as to give reasonable cause to believe that an order under this section is necessary to protect the public from serious harm to him;

the chief officer may apply for an order under this section to be made in respect of the person.

Ss (2)

Such an application shall be made by complaint to the relevant magistrates' court within whose **'commission area'** it is alleged that the defendant acted in such a way as is mentioned in Sub-section (1)(b) above.

Ss (3)

If, on such an application, it is proved that the conditions mentioned in Sub-section (1) above are fulfilled, the magistrates' court may make an order under this section - **'a sex offender order'** - which prohibits the defendant from doing anything described in the order.

Ss (4)
The prohibitions which may be imposed by a sex offender order are those necessary for the purpose of protecting the public from serious harm from the defendant.

Ss (5)
A sex offender order shall have effect for a period (not less than five years) specified in the order - or until a further order is made. While such an order has effect, Sections 1 - 3 Sex Offenders Act 1997 (notification and registration requirements for sex offenders - see 3.34) shall have effect as if:

(a) the defendant was subject to the notification requirements of that Part of the Act; and

(b) in relation to the defendant, the relevant date - within the meaning of that Part of the Act (see 3.34, Section 1(8)) - were the date of the service of the order.

Ss (6)
Subject to Sub-section (7) below, the applicant or the defendant may apply by complaint - to the court that made the sex offender order - for it to be varied or discharged by further order.

Ss (7)
Except with the consent of both parties, no sex offender order shall be discharged before the end of the period of five years beginning with the date of service of the order.

Ss (8)
If, without reasonable excuse, a person does anything that she or he is prohibited from doing by a sex offender order, she or he shall be liable:

(a) on summary conviction, to imprisonment for a term not exceeding six months or to a fine not exceeding the statutory maximum or to both; or

(b) on conviction on indictment, to imprisonment for a term not exceeding five years, or to a fine,, or to both.

Ss (9)
If a person is convicted of an offence under Sub-section (8) above, it shall not be open to the court by or before which she or he is so convicted, to make an order for conditional discharge in respect of the offence.

Notes

See Section 3(2) (following page) for a definition of the **'relevant date'**.

'Commission area' is the area for which a magistrates' court is responsible - therefore the application should be made to that magistrates' court responsible for the area in which the offence is alleged to have been committed.

Section 3

Ss (1)
In this Section and in Section 2 of the Act, **'sex offender'** means a person who:

(a) has been convicted of an offence to which Part I (Sections 1 - 3) of the Sex Offenders Act 1997 applies (see 3.34);

(b) has been found not guilty by reason of insanity or found to be under a disability and to have done the act charged against her or him in respect of such an offence;

(c) has been cautioned by a constable in England and Wales or Northern Ireland in respect of such an offence which, at the time when the caution was given, she or he had admitted; or

(d) has been punished under the law in force in a country or territory outside the United Kingdom for an act which:
  (i) constituted an offence under the law of that country or territory; and
  (ii) would have constituted a sexual offence to which Part I Sex Offenders Act 1997 applies if it had been done in any part of the United Kingdom.

Ss (2)
In Section 2(1) (previous page) the **'relevant date'** in relation to a sex offender means:

(a) the date or, as the case may be, the latest date on which she or he has been convicted, found, cautioned or punished as mentioned in Sub-section (1) above; or

(b) if later, the date of the commencement of that Section (December 1, 1998).

Ss (3)

Sub-sections (2) and (3) of Section 6 of the Sex Offenders Act 1997* apply to the **'construction of references'** to Sub-sections (1) and (2) of this Section as they apply to the construction of references to Part I of the Sex Offenders Act 1997.

* Ss 6(2)and(3) Sex Offenders Act concern the way **'conviction'** and **'disability'** are defined (see Notes at the end of this Section).

Ss (4)

In Sub-sections (1) and (2) above, any reference to a person having been cautioned shall be construed as including a reference to her or his having been reprimanded or warned under Section 65 of the Crime and Disorder Act 1998 **.

** Section 65 Crime and Disorder Act 1998 provides for the reprimand and warning of young offenders by police.

Ss (5)

An act punishable under the law in force in any country or territory outside the United Kingdom constitutes an offence under that law for the purposes of Sub-section (1).

Ss (6)

Subject to Sub-section (7), the condition in Sub-section (1)(d)(i) shall be taken to be satisfied unless - not later than the rules of court may provide - the defendant serves on the applicant a notice:

(a) stating that, on the facts as alleged with respect to the act in question, the condition is not in her or his opinion satisfied;

(b) showing her or his grounds for that opinion; and

(c) requiring the applicant to show that it is satisfied.

Ss (7)

The court, if it thinks fit, may permit the defendant to require the applicant to show that the condition is satisfied without the prior service of a notice under Sub-section (6).

Notes

Sections 2 to 4 of the Crime and Disorder Act 1998 came into force on 1.12.98.

References to a **'conviction'** include:

- findings in summary proceedings in which the court makes an order under Section 37(3) Mental Health Act 1983, Section 58(3) Criminal Procedure (Scotland) Act 1995 or Article 44(4) Mental Health (Northern Ireland) order 1986, that the accused did the act charged; and
- findings in summary proceedings in Scotland in which the court makes an order that the accused committed the offence - but discharging her or him absolutely under Section 246(3) Criminal Procedure (Scotland) Act 1995.

References to a person having been found to be under a **'disability'** and to have done the act charged in respect of a sexual offence to which this part of the Act applies, include references to her or him having been found unfit to be tried for such an offence, to be insane so that the trial can proceed, or to be unfit to be tried.

The **'construction of references'** refers to instances in which the concepts of 'conviction' and 'being found to be under a disability' are used in Section 3 (1) and (2) Crime and Disorder Act 1998. Where these concepts are used, they should be defined as in the previous Note re 'conviction' and disability'.

Section 4

Ss (1)

An appeal can be made to the Crown court against the making of a sex offender order by a magistrates' court.

Ss (2)

On such an appeal the Crown court:

(a) may make such orders as may be necessary to ensure that its decision is put into effect; and

(b) may also make such incidental or consequential orders as appear to it to be just.

Ss (3)

Any order of the Crown court made on an appeal under this Section (other than one directing that an application be re-heard by a magistrates' court) shall - for the purposes of Section 2(6) of this Act (ante) - be treated as if it were an order of the magistrates' court from which the appeal was brought, and not an order of the Crown court.

CHAPTER 4

PHYSICAL ABUSE

4.1. Murder

> 'Murder is when a person unlawfully kills another human being under the Queen's peace and with malice aforethought' (Murphy 1998).
>
> Contrary to Common Law

Notes

'Unlawfully' refers to the killing taking place in circumstances other than:

a. those in which the force used was **'reasonable'** being 'no more then absolutely necessary' in preventing crime or effecting or assisting in a lawful arrest (Section 3 Criminal Law Act 1967 and Article 2 ECHR) (see Chapter 10);
b. those in which the force used was 'no more than absolutely necessary' in self defence or in defence of another. Causing the death of another, solely for the protection of property, cannot be justified under ECHR Article 2 (Right to Life);
c. those in which the death occurred as a result of misadventure (for example, during a lawful medical operation carried out by a surgeon with proper care (English and Card 1994)).

In order to support a charge of murder, the prosecution will need to prove that the accused had the intention to either kill or cause grievous bodily harm (such an intention is commonly referred to as **'malice aforethought'**).

The concept of murder originally included the idea that the victim's death would need to take place within a year and a day of the injury being sustained. This requirement was abolished by the Law Reform (Year and a Day Rule) Act 1996 and applies to acts or omissions committed on or after 26.6.96.

In cases in which the necessary elements of murder are present, the mitigating factors set out below might reduce the offence to one of manslaughter:

a. provocation;
b. diminished responsibility;
c. suicide pact.

'Provocation' refers to a loss of self control on the part of the accused as a result of things said or done. The question of if what was said and/or done was enough to make a reasonable person lose self control is a matter for the jury in determining whether provocation may be said to have taken place (Section 3 Homicide Act 1957).

'Diminished responsibility' refers to an 'abnormality of the mind (whether arising from a condition of arrested or retarded development or any inherent causes, or induced by disease or injury)' that is such as to 'substantially impair' the accused's 'mental responsibility for her or his Acts or omissions in doing or being party to the killing' (Section 2(1) Homicide Act 1957). The burden of proving diminished responsibility rests with the defence (Section 2(2) Homicide Act 1957).

'Suicide pact' refers to a 'common agreement between two or more persons – having for its object the death of all of them – whether or not each is to take his or her own life'. In these circumstances, the actions of the accused in killing or in being party to the killing of another by a third person are only mitigated if she or he acted in pursuance of an agreement with the victim to do so AND had the intention of dying her or himself in accordance with that agreement at the time of the killing (Sections 4(1) and 4(3) Homicide Act 1957). The burden of proving that the killing took place in pursuit of such a suicide pact rests with the defence (Section 4(2) Homicide Act 1957).

Punishable

on indictment with life imprisonment (mandatory).

4.2. Manslaughter

> Manslaughter is committed – when an unlawful homicide takes place – in circumstances in which the intention to kill or cause grievous bodily harm – is mitigated by provocation, diminished responsibility or a suicide pact (voluntary manslaughter) – or in circumstances in which the intention to kill or cause grievous bodily harm was absent (involuntary manslaughter).
>
> Contrary to Common Law

Notes

'Unlawful' has the same meaning as in Murder (referred to as **'unlawfully'** - see 4.1).

'Provocation', **'diminished responsibility'** and **'suicide pact'** are defined with reference to Murder (previous page).

'Involuntary manslaughter' falls into two categories – constructive manslaughter and manslaughter by breach of duty.

Constructive manslaughter refers to the doing of an unlawful and dangerous act that is likely to cause harm and result in death.

Manslaughter by breach of duty refers to circumstances in which a person is killed as a result of another's gross negligence in doing or failing to do an act when she or he is under a duty to take care of the health or safety of others (English and Card 1994).

Punishable

on indictment with life imprisonment.

4.3. Infanticide

> When any woman – by any wilful act or omission – causes the death of her child – being a child under the age of 12 months – but at the time of the act or omission the balance of her mind was disturbed by reason of her not having fully recovered from the effect of giving birth to the child or by reason of the effect of lactation consequent to the birth of the child – then – notwithstanding that the circumstances were such that but for this fact the offence would have amounted to one of murder – she shall be guilty of infanticide and may for such offence be dealt with and punished as if she had been guilty of the offence of manslaughter of the child.
>
> Section 1 Infanticide Act 1938

Example

A charge under this Section could be considered if a woman causes the death of her baby, either by wilful assault or neglect, while suffering from the effects of post-natal depression to the point that it could be said that her responsibility for the behaviour was diminished.

Punishable

on indictment with life imprisonment.

4.4. Threats to kill

> A person who, without lawful excuse – makes to another a threat – intending that that other would fear it would be carried out – to kill that other or a third person – shall be guilty of an offence.
>
> Section 16 Offences Against the Person Act 1861

Note

A lawful excuse may exist when the threat was **'reasonable'** in self defence (Attorney General's Reference No 2 of 1983, 1 All ER 988 of 1984) or in preventing crime (Section 3 Criminal Law Act 1967).

Example

A charge under this Section could be considered if a threat to kill is made to a child – intending that that child would fear that the threat would be carried out – irrespective of whether or not the accused person actually intends to carry out that threat.

Punishable

on indictment with 10 years' imprisonment.

4.5. Grievous bodily harm or wounding with intent

> It is an offence to unlawfully and maliciously, by any means whatsoever – wound or cause any grievous bodily harm to any person – with intent to do some grievous bodily harm to any person – or with intent to resist or prevent the lawful apprehension or detainer (detention) of any person.
>
> Section 18 Offences Against the Person Act 1861

Notes

Unlawfully' refers to circumstances other than:

(a) those in which the force was 'reasonable' being 'no more than absolutely necessary' in preventing crime or effecting or assisting in a lawful arrest (Section 3 Criminal law Act 1967 and Article 2 ECHR) (See Chapter 10)

(b) those in which the force used was no more than absolutely necessary in self defence or in defence of another. Causing the death of another, solely for the protection of property, cannot be justified under ECHR Article 2 (Right to Life).

'Maliciously' in this context refers to circumstances in which the defendant either intends to cause harm to some person or is reckless as to the possibility of it – in the sense of having foreseen the harm that might result from her or his behaviour – and yet gone on to take the risk of its occurrence (Draycott and Carr 1998).

'Wound' means that there must be a break in the continuity of the whole skin (an injury in which there has merely been internal rupturing of blood vessels is not a 'wound') (*C v Eisenhower* 1984 3 All ER 230).

'Grievous bodily harm' means really serious harm – for example, broken bones might fall into this category of injury (Crown Prosecution Service Charging Standards for Offences Against the Person).

'Intent' means that the defendant must have actually intended one of the specified objectives of the action. Recklessness cannot amount to the specific intent required (*R v Belfon* 1976 3 All ER 46).

Punishable

on indictment with life imprisonment.

4.6. Grievous bodily harm or wounding

> It is an offence to unlawfully and maliciously wound or inflict grievous bodily harm upon any person either with or without any weapon or instrument.
>
> Section 20 Offences Against the Person Act 1861

Notes

'Unlawfully', **'maliciously'**, **'wound'** and **'grievous bodily harm'** have the same meaning as in Grievous Bodily Harm or Wounding with Intent (above).

Punishable

on indictment with five years' imprisonment.

4.7. Attempting to choke etc so as to commit an indictable offence

> Any person who, by any means – attempts to choke, suffocate or strangle any other person – or who attempts to render any other person insensible, unconscious or incapable of resistance – with intent to enable her or himself or any other person to commit any indictable offence – or with intent to assist any other person in committing any indictable offence – shall be guilty of an offence.
>
> Section 21 Offences Against the Person Act 1861

Example

Suffocating a child with a view to raping her or buggering her or him might amount to an offence under this Section.

Punishable

on indictment with life imprisonment.

4.8. Using chloroform etc so as to commit an indictable offence

> Any person who unlawfully applies to – or administers to or causes to be taken by or attempts to apply to or administer to, or attempts to cause to be administered to or taken by – any person – any chloroform, laudanum or other stupefying or overpowering drug, matter or thing – with intent in any such case to enable her or himself or any other person to commit any indictable offence – or with intent to assist any other person in committing any indictable offence – shall be guilty of an offence.
>
> Section 22 Offences Against the Person Act 1861

Example

A charge under this Section could be considered if a person administers a drug to a child with a view to committing an indecent act with her or him or another person.

Punishable

on indictment with life imprisonment.

4.9. Maliciously administering poison etc so as to endanger life etc

> Any person who unlawfully and maliciously administers to or causes to be administered to or taken by any other person – any poison or other destructive or noxious thing – so as thereby to endanger the life of such a person or so as to inflict upon any person any grievous bodily harm, shall be guilty of an offence.
>
> Section 23 Offences Against the Person Act 1861

Example

A charge under this Section could be considered if a person maliciously administered a poison to a child with a view to endangering the life of that child.

Punishable

on indictment with 10 years' imprisonment.

4.10. Maliciously administering poison etc with intent to injure, aggrieve or annoy

> Any person who unlawfully and maliciously administers to or causes to be administered to or taken by any other person – any poison or other destructive or noxious thing – with intent to injure, aggrieve or annoy such a person – shall be guilty of an offence.
>
> Section 24 Offences Against the Person Act 1861

Example

A charge under this Section could be considered if a person causes a child to drink some kind of poisonous substance with a view to injuring (though not killing) her or him.

Punishable

on indictment with five years' imprisonment.

4.11. Assault occasioning actual bodily harm

> It is an offence to assault a person, thereby occasioning that person actual bodily harm.
>
> Section 47 Offences Against the Person Act 1861

Notes

'Assault' has the same meaning as in Common Assault and Battery (below).

'Actual bodily harm' means some form of hurt or injury calculated to interfere with the health or comfort of another. It need not be permanent, but must be more than merely transient or trifling – a bruise is sufficient, a minor and transient reddening of the skin sustained as a result of a hand slap might not be. Actual bodily harm can include psychiatric injury (*R v Ireland* 1997 3 All ER 225) but it must go beyond simple emotions such as fear or panic (*R v Chan-Fook* 1994 2 All ER 552).

Punishable

on indictment with five years' imprisonment.

4.12. Common assault and battery

> It is an offence to assault a person.
>
> Section 39 Criminal Justice Act 1988

Notes

The term **'assault'** is taken to mean either an assault by threats or an assault by beating (*DPP v Taylor, DPP v Little* 1992 1 All ER 299). An assault by threats is committed by a person who intentionally or recklessly causes another person to fear immediate and unlawful personal violence (*R v Venna* 1976 3 All ER 788). An assault by beating (often referred to as a **'battery'**) takes place if unlawful personal violence is actually used, regardless of whether the victim is put in fear or not (*R v Rolfe* 1952 36 CR App R4).

There are a number of defences to an assault:

'Consent' – a person may only give valid consent to a common assault in the case of consenting to reasonable medical procedures or within the confines of the rules of a lawful game, ie boxing (English and Card 1994).

'Lawful chastisement of a child', corporal punishment and 'parental chastisement' - All forms of corporal punishment are banned in local authority, special and grant-maintained schools in the UK (Section 548(1) Education Act 1996). There was a defence, in UK common law, of 'parental chastisement' against a charge of assault where a parent had smacked their child. This defence allowed a parent to cause reasonable pain and discomfort to a child during the chastisement, but not 'actual bodily harm'. The UK common law defence allowed parents to inflict 'moderate and reasonable' chastisement on their children. When reviewing a case, the European Court of Human Rights held that the defence of lawful chastisement was too wide and failed to protect children adequately; it should therefore be amended. (Also see Chapter 10.)

'Lawful authority' in preventing crime or in effecting a lawful arrest. The extent to which such an assault may be considered lawful depends upon what is **'reasonable'** in the circumstances (Section 3 Criminal Law Act 1967).

'Self-defence, defence of property, defence of another' – again, the extent to which such an assault may be considered lawful depends upon what is **'reasonable'** in the circumstances (Attorney General's Reference No 2 of 1983, 1 All ER 988 of 1984 and *R v Duffy* 1966 1 All ER 62).

Punishable

on a summary basis only with six months' imprisonment.

4.13. Prohibition of female circumcision

Except when done for physical or mental health reasons – by a registered medical health practitioner – or upon a person who is in labour or who has just given birth – and for reasons connected with such labour or birth – by a registered medical practitioner, registered midwife – or by a person undergoing a course of training with a view to becoming a registered medical practitioner or a registered midwife – it shall be an offence for any person:

a. to excise (ie cut off or out), infibulate (ie fasten with a clasp) or otherwise mutilate the whole or any part of the labia majora, labia minora or clitoris of any other person; or
b. to aid, abet, counsel or procure the performance by any other person of any of those acts on that other person's own body.

Prohibition of Female Circumcision Act 1985

Note

Most local authorities have developed local procedures for dealing with allegations of this particular offence in response to guidance from the Department of Health.

Example

This offence is committed by the individual who actually conducts such an operation, by any person assisting in it and by any other person counselling or procuring it (for example a child's parents or guardians).

Punishable

on indictment with five years' imprisonment.

FIG 5: PHYSICAL ASSAULTS ON CHILDREN

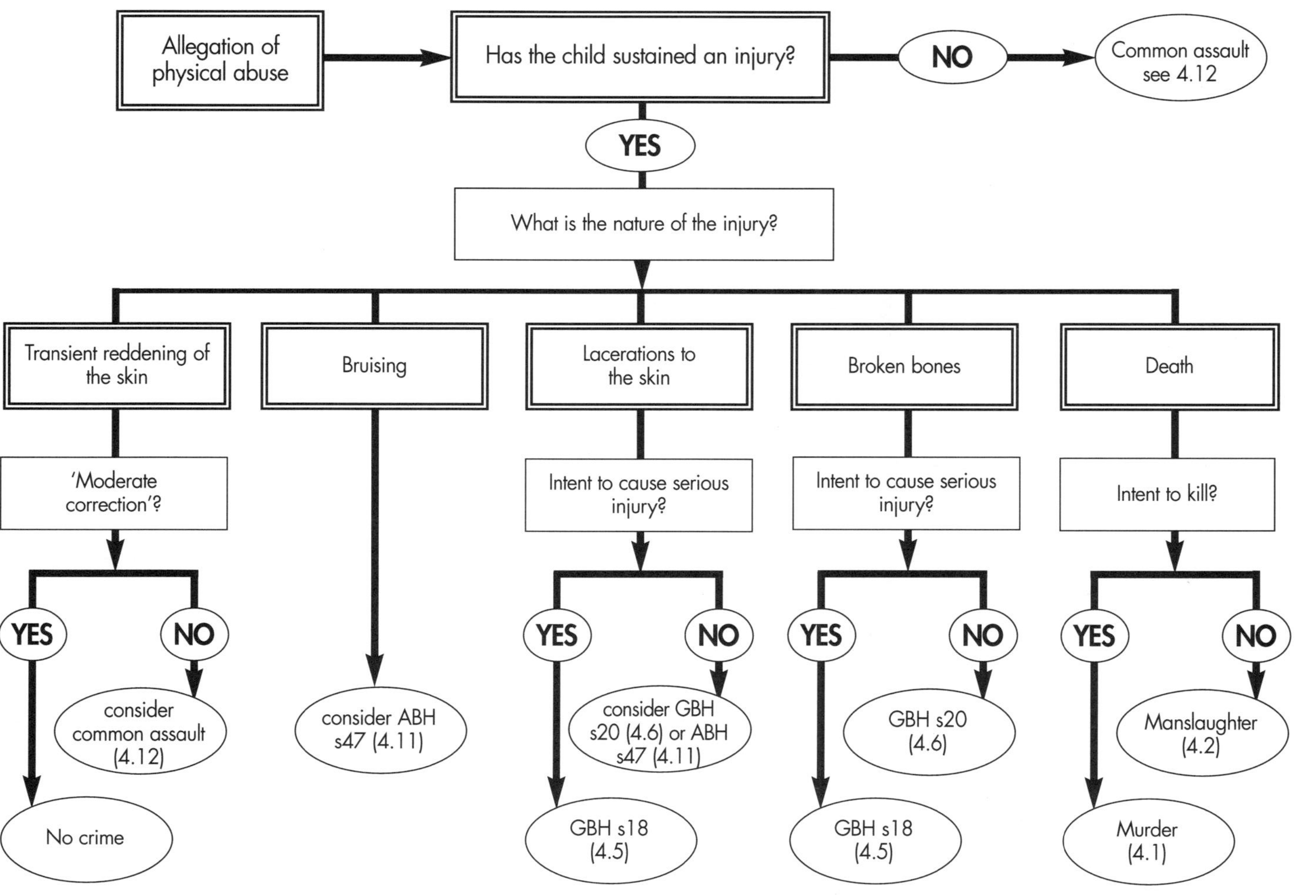

CHAPTER 5

CRUELTY AND NEGLECT

5.1 Cruelty to children

5.1a. Wilful assault

> It is an offence for a person who has attained the age of 16 years, and who has responsibility for any child or young person under that age - to wilfully assault such a child or young person, or to cause or procure her or him to be assaulted - in a manner likely to cause her or him unnecessary suffering or injury to health (including injury to or loss of sight, hearing, limb or organ of the body, and any mental derangement).
>
> Section 1 Children and Young Persons Act 1933

Notes

'Child' means a person under the age of 14 years (Section 107 Children and Young Persons Act 1933 as amended by the Children Act 1989).

'Young person' means a person who has attained the age of 14 years but is under the age of 18 years - 16 years for the purposes of this particular Section - (Section 107 Children and Young Persons Act 1933 as amended by the Children Act 1989).

'Responsibility' means:

a. having **'parental responsibility'** for that child or young person within the meaning of the Children Act 1989 (natural mother - natural father if the mother and father were married to each other at the time of the child or young person's birth - natural father if a **'parental responsibility agreement'** has been drawn up in the form prescribed by the Lord Chancellor - and any person having parental responsibility by virtue of some form of court order);
b. otherwise being legally liable to maintain that child or young person;
c. otherwise having the care of that child or young person;

(Section 17(1) Children and Young Persons Act 1933.)

A person responsible for a child or young person by virtue of (a.) above will not have ceased to have responsibility for her or him simply because she or he does not have care of her or him (Section 17(2) Children and Young Persons Act 1933).

'Wilfully' means a deliberate or reckless act or failure. A genuine lack of appreciation through stupidity, ignorance or personal inadequacy will be a good defence. The offence is not to be judged by what a reasonable parent would have done (*R v Sheppard* 1981 3 All ER 899).

'Assault'. A common assault would not be sufficient in itself to prove a charge under this Section. It would rather need to include - or to be likely to give rise to - unnecessary suffering or injury to health.

Example

A charge could be considered under this Section if the child has been tied to a chair for several hours, causing the child considerable unnecessary suffering.

Punishable

on indictment with 10 years' imprisonment.

5.1b. Wilful ill-treatment

> It is an offence for a person who has attained the age of 16 years - and who has responsibility for any child or young person under that age - to wilfully ill-treat such a child or young person, or to cause or procure her or him to be ill-treated - in a manner likely to cause her or him unnecessary suffering or injury to health (including injury to or loss of sight, hearing, limb or organ of the body, and any mental derangement).
>
> Section 1 Children and Young Persons Act 1933

Notes

'Child', **'young person'**, **'responsibility'** and **'wilful'** have the same meaning as in Wilful Assault (see 5.1).

'Ill-treat' may be established if a course of conduct, which would not in isolation be serious enough to justify criminal proceedings, is repeated over an inordinate length of time (Lyon and De Cruz 1993).

Example

Conduct sufficient for ill-treatment could amount to a series of assaults over a period of time.

Punishable

on indictment with 10 years' imprisonment.

5.1c. Wilful neglect

> It is an offence for a person who has attained the age of 16 years - and who has responsibility for any child or young person under that age - to wilfully neglect such a child or young person - or to cause or procure her or him to be neglected - in a manner likely to cause her or him unnecessary suffering or injury to health (including injury to or loss of sight, hearing, limb or organ of the body, and any mental derangement).
>
> Section 1 Children and Young Persons Act 1933

Notes

'Child', **'young person'**, **'responsibility'** and **'wilful'** have the same meaning as in Wilful Assault (previous page).

'Neglect' - under this Section, a child or young person will be deemed to have been neglected if:

a. a parent or other person legally liable to maintain a child or young person, or the legal guardian of a child or young person - shall be deemed to have neglected her or him in a manner likely to cause injury to her or his health - if she or he has failed to provide adequate food, clothing, medical aid or lodging for her or him or if, having been unable otherwise to provide such food, clothing, medical aid or lodging, she or he has failed to take steps to procure it to be provided under the enactments made for these purposes;
b. it is proved that the death of an infant under three years of age was caused by suffocation (not being suffocation caused by disease or any foreign body in the throat or air passages of the infant) - while the infant was in bed with some other person who had attained the age of 16 years - and that other person was, when she or he went to bed, under the influence of drink - then that other person will be deemed to have neglected the infant in a manner likely to cause injury to its health;

(Section 1(2) Children and Young Persons Act 1933).

'Likely to cause unnecessary suffering or injury to health' in respect of wilful neglect includes a deliberate omission to supply medical treatment (Section 1(2) Children and Young Persons Act 1933). However, direct evidence of unnecessary suffering or injury to health is not strictly necessary because these elements of the offence may be inferred from evidence of the impact of neglect on the child or young person (*R v Brenton* 1904 111 CCC Sess Rep 309). The effect of the action of another person in relieving suffering, injury etc, provides no defence to a charge under this Section, (Section 1(3) Children and young Persons Act 1933).

Example
A caregiver's failure to seek medical/psychiatric help for a child whom she or he knows to be in need of such treatment, and this failure being despite a knowledge that the probable consequences of her or his failure might amount to an offence under this Section.

Punishable
on indictment with 10 years' imprisonment.

5.1d. Wilful abandonment

> It is an offence for a person who has attained the age of 16 years - and who has responsibility for any child or young person under that age - to wilfully abandon` such a child or young person, or to cause or procure her or him to be abandoned - in a manner likely to cause her or him unnecessary suffering or injury to health (including injury to or loss of sight, hearing, limb or organ of the body, and any mental derangement).
>
> Section 1 Children and Young Persons Act 1933

Notes
'Child', **'young person'**, **'responsibility'** and **'wilful'** have the same meaning as in Wilful Assault (see 5.1).

'Abandon' means leaving a child or young person to its fate (*R v Boulden* 1957 41 CR App Rep 105).

Example
A charge under this Section might be considered if a child is left by a caregiver who has no intention of returning for the child.

Punishable
on indictment with 10 years' imprisonment.

5.1e. Wilful exposure

> It is an offence for a person who has attained the age of 16 years - and who has responsibility for any child or young person under that age - to wilfully expose such a child or young person, or to cause or procure her or him to be exposed - in a manner likely to cause her or him unnecessary suffering or injury to health (including injury to or loss of sight, hearing, limb or organ of the body, and any mental derangement).
>
> Section 1 Children and Young Persons Act 1933

Notes
'Child', **'young person'**, **'responsibility'** and **'wilful'** have the same meaning as in Wilful Assault (see 5.1).

'Expose' means to expose to the likelihood of unnecessary suffering or injury to health. There is no necessity for the physical placing of a child or young person somewhere with intent to injure it (*R v Williams* 1910 74 JPJo 99 as cited in Draycott and Carr 1998).

Example
Provided the requisite element of wilfulness is present, this offence could be considered if young children are left without baby sitters by parents who stay out until the early hours at public houses or clubs.

Punishable
on indictment with 10 years' imprisonment.

FIG 6: CHILD CRUELTY

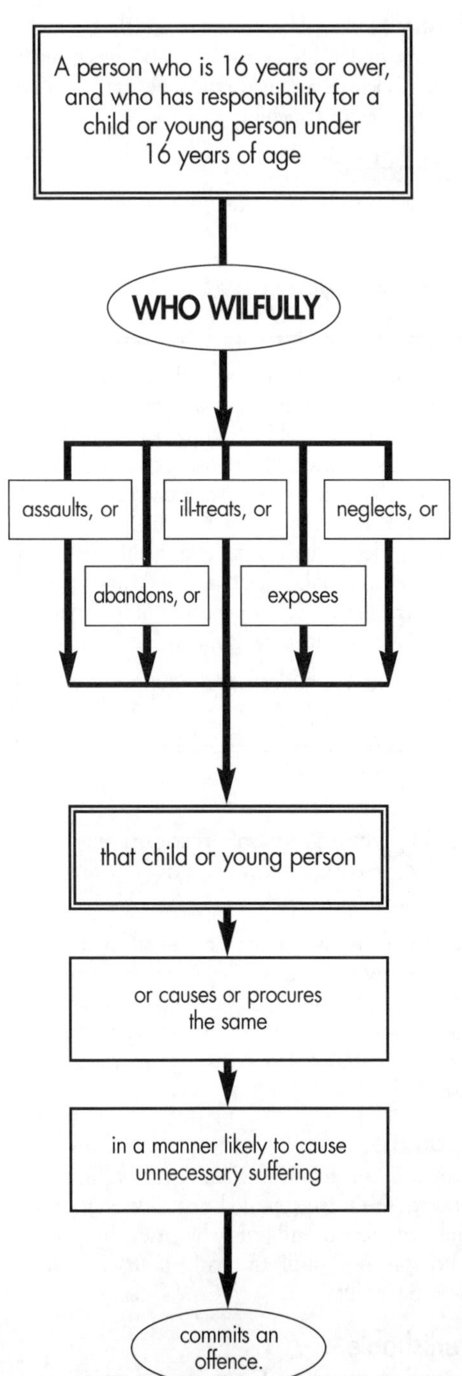

5.2. Exposing a child whereby life is in danger

> Any person who unlawfully abandons or exposes any child under the age of two years - whereby the life of the child is endangered or the health of the child has or is likely to have been permanently injured - shall be guilty of an offence.
>
> Section 27 Offences Against the Person Act 1861

Punishable
on indictment with five years' imprisonment.

5.3. Drunk in charge of a child apparently under the age of seven years

> If any person is found drunk - in any highway or other public place whether a building or not, or on any licensed premises - while having the charge of a child apparently under the age of seven years - she or he shall be guilty of an offence.
>
> Section 2(1) Licensing Act 1902

Note

A child will be deemed to be under the age of seven years if she or he appears to the court to be under that age unless the contrary is proved (Section 2(2) Licensing Act 1902).

Punishable
on a summary basis only, with one month's imprisonment.

CHAPTER 6

OFFENCES RELATING TO PREGNANCY

6.1. Child destruction

> Any person who - by any wilful act - with intent to destroy the life of a child capable of being born alive - causes a child to die before it has an existence independent of its mother - shall be guilty of child destruction.
>
> Section 1(1) Infant Life (Preservation) Act 1929

Note

For the purposes of this Act, evidence that a woman had at any material time been pregnant for a period of 28 weeks or more shall be *prima facie* proof that she was at that time pregnant of a child capable of being born alive (Section 1(1) Infant Life (Preservation) Act 1929).

Under human rights law, abortion raises issues under Article 2 (Right to Life) and Article 8 (Right to Respect for Private and Family Life) of ECHR. Decided cases have held that the foetus has no 'absolute right' to life, therefore a lawful medical abortion cannot be an infringement of rights.

Example

A charge under this Section might be considered if a person kills an unborn child after 28 weeks' gestation as a result of trying to terminate the pregnancy.

Punishable

on indictment with life imprisonment.

6.2. Administering drugs/using instruments to procure abortion

> Any woman being with child who - with intent to procure her own miscarriage - unlawfully administers to herself any poison or other noxious thing - or unlawfully uses any instrument or other means whatsoever with the like intent - shall be guilty of an offence and;
>
> whosoever, with intent to procure the miscarriage of any woman - whether she be or be not with child - unlawfully administers to her or causes to be taken by her any poison or other noxious thing - or unlawfully uses any instrument or other means whatsoever with the like intent - shall be guilty of an offence.
>
> Section 58 Offences Against the Person Act 1861

Notes

When a woman is charged with this offence it is necessary to show that she was in fact pregnant. If she was not in fact pregnant, she may be guilty of an attempt to commit this offence.

Taking a thing in the belief that it is capable of causing an abortion, even though it was not in fact capable of producing such an effect, may amount to an attempt to commit this offence.

Punishable

on indictment with imprisonment for life.

6.3. Procuring drugs etc to cause abortion

> Whosoever shall unlawfully supply or procure - any poison or other noxious thing - or any instrument or thing whatsoever - knowing that the same is intended to be unlawfully used or employed with intent to procure the miscarriage of any woman - whether she be or not be with child - shall be guilty of an offence.
>
> Section 59 Offences Against the Person Act 1861

Punishable

on indictment with five years' imprisonment

6.4. Concealing the birth of a child

> If any woman shall be delivered of a child - every person - who by any secret disposition of the body of the said child - whether the child died before, at or after its birth - endeavours to conceal the birth thereof - shall be guilty of an offence.
>
> Section 60 Offences Against the Person Act 1861

Note

'Conceal' refers to a desire to keep the world at large in ignorance of the birth and not from a desire to escape individual anger (*R v Morris* 1848 2 Cox CC 489).

Example

A charge under this Section might be considered if the dead body of a child is deliberately hidden with a view to keeping the authorities ignorant of the death of that child.

Punishable

on indictment with two years' imprisonment

Other relevant offences might be

(a) making a false statement as to any birth or death (Section 4 Perjury Act 1911);

(b) failing to give information concerning a birth or death when under a statutory duty to do so (Section 36 Births and Deaths Registration Act 1953);

(c) disposing of or destroying a dead body to prevent an inquest being held (common law offence).

CHAPTER 7

ABDUCTION

See also the offences of abduction under the Sexual Offences Act 1956 (3.20-3.23).

7.1. Child abduction by a person connected with the child

Section 1 Child Abduction Act 1984 (as amended by Family Law Act 1986 and the Children Act 1989)

Ss (1)

Subject to Sub-sections (5) and (8) below, a person **'connected with a child'*** under the age of 16 years commits an offence if she or he takes or sends the child out of the United Kingdom without the **'appropriate consent'****.

* ** See Ss (2) and (3) below.

Ss (2)

A person is **'connected with a child'** for the purposes of this Section if:

(a) she or he is the parent of the child; or

(b) in the case of a child whose parents were not married at the time of the child's birth, there are reasonable grounds for believing him to be the father of the child; or

(c) she or he is the **'guardian of the child'**; or

(d) she or he is a person in whose favour a **'residence order'** is in force with respect to the child; or

(e) she or he has **'custody of the child'**.

Ss (3)

The **'appropriate consent'** in relation to a child means:

(a) the consent of the following -
  i. the child's mother,
  ii. the child's father, if he has **'parental responsibility'** for her or him,
  iii. any guardian of the child,
  iv. any person in whose favour a residence order is in force with respect to the child,
  v. any person who has custody of the child, or

(b) the leave of the court granted by virtue of a provision of Part II of the Children Act 1989 (residence, contact, prohibited steps, specific issues, financial relief and financial assistance orders); or

(c) if any person has custody of the child, the leave of the court which awarded custody of that child.

Ss (4)

A person does not commit an offence under this Section (see provisos in Ss (4A) below) by taking or sending a child out of the United Kingdom without obtaining the appropriate consent if:

(a) she or he is a person in whose favour there is a residence order in force with respect to the child; and

(b) she or he takes or sends the child out of the United Kingdom for a period less than one month.

Ss (4A)

The above Sub-section does not apply if the person taking or sending the child out of the United Kingdom does so in breach of an order under Part II of the Children Act 1989.

Ss (5)

A person does not commit an offence under this Section by doing anything without the consent of another person whose consent is required under the foregoing provisions if:

(a) she or he does it in the belief that the other person -
  i. has consented,
  ii. would consent if she or he was aware of all the relevant circumstances, or

(b) she or he has taken all reasonable steps to communicate with that other person; or

(c) the other person has unreasonably refused to consent (see provisos in Ss (5A) bellow).

Ss (5A)
Paragraph (c) of Sub-section (5) does not apply if:

(a) the person who refused to consent is a person -
  i. in whose favour there is a residence order in force with respect to the child, or
  ii. who has custody of the child, or

(b) the person taking or sending the child out of the United Kingdom is, by so acting, in breach of an order made by a court in the UK.

Ss (6)
If, in proceedings for an offence under this Section, there is sufficient evidence to raise an issue as to the application of Sub-section (5) above, it shall be for the prosecution to prove that the Sub-section does not apply.

Ss (7)
For the purposes of this Section:

(a) **'Guardian of a child'**, **'residence order'** and **'parental responsibility'** have the same meaning as in the Children Act 1989. Residence order is defined in Residence, Contact and Other Orders (see 2.5) and parental responsibility is defined in the Notes to Chapter 1, Police Protection (see 1.1).

  A **'guardian of a child'** is either appointed by a court - or appointed by a parent with parental responsibility, or by another guardian, on her or his death - in a will or in a document that has been formally witnessed.

(b) A person shall be treated as having **'custody of a child'** if there is in force an order of a court in the United Kingdom awarding her or him (whether solely or jointly with another person) custody, legal custody or care and control of the child.

Ss (8)
This Section shall have effect subject to the provisions of the Schedule to this Act in relation to a child who is in the care of a local authority, detained in a place of safety, remanded to a local authority accommodation, or the subject of proceedings or an order relating to adoption.

Punishable
on indictment with seven years' imprisonment.

7.2. Child abduction by other persons

Section 2 Child Abduction Act 1984 (as amended by the Children Act 1989)

Ss (1)
Subject to Sub-section (3) below, a person other than one mentioned in Sub-section (2) below commits an offence if, without lawful authority or reasonable excuse, she or he takes or detains a child under the age of 16 years:

(a) so as to remove that child from the lawful control of any person having lawful control of the child; or

(b) so as to keep the child out of the lawful control of any person entitled to lawful control of the child.

Ss (2)
The persons exempt from Sub-section (1) are:

(a) when the father and mother of the child in question were married to each other at the time of her or his birth - the child's father and mother

(b) when the father and mother of the child in question were not married to each other at the time of her or his birth - the child's mother; and

(c) any other person mentioned in Section 1(2)(c) to (e) of this Act (previous page).

Ss (3)
In proceedings against any person for an offence under this Section, it shall be a defence for that person to prove:

(a) when the father and mother of the child in question were not married to each other at the time of the child's birth -
  i. that he is the child's father; or
  ii. that, at the time of the alleged offence, he believed on reasonable grounds that he was the child's father;

(b) that, at the time of the alleged offence, she or he believed that the child had attained the age of 16 years.

Punishable
on indictment with seven years' imprisonment.

7.3. Abduction of children in care etc

Section 49 Children Act 1989

Ss (1)

A person shall be guilty of an offence if, knowingly and without lawful authority or reasonable excuse, she or he:

(a) takes a child to whom this Section applies away from the responsible person;

(b) keeps such a child away from the responsible person; or

(c) induces, assists or incites such a child to run away or stay away from the responsible person.

Ss (2)

This Section applies in relation to a child who is:

(a) in care;

(b) the subject of an emergency protection order; or

(c) in police protection.

Notes

'Responsible person' means any person who for the time being has care of the child by virtue of a care order, an emergency protection order or police protection.

Punishable

on a summary basis only, with six months' imprisonment.

PART THREE

POLICE POWERS

CHAPTER 8

POWERS OF ARREST

8.1. Arrestable offences

Section 24 Police and Criminal Evidence Act 1984 (as amended by the Sexual Offences Act 1985, the Criminal Justice Act 1988, the Official Secrets Act 1989, the Football (Offences) Act 1991 and the Criminal Justice and Public Order Act 1994)

Ss (1)

The powers of summary arrest conferred by the following Sub-sections shall apply:

(a) to offences for which the sentence is fixed by law;

(b) to offences for which a person of 21 years of age or over (not previously convicted) may be sentenced to imprisonment for a term of five years (or might be so sentenced but for the restrictions imposed by Section 33 of the Magistrates' Courts Act 1980); and

(c) to the offences to which Sub-section (2) below applied;

and in this Act **'arrestable offence'** means any such offence.

Ss (2)

The offences to which this Sub-section applies are:

(a) offences for which a person may be arrested under the Customs and Excise Act – as defined in Section 11 of the Customs and Excise Management Act 1979;

(b) offences under the Official Secrets Act 1920 that are not arrestable offences by virtue of the term of imprisonment for which a person may be sentenced in respect of them – and offences under the Official Secrets Act 1989 except Sections 8(1), 8(4) or 8(5);

(c) offences under Sections 22 (causing prostitution of women) or 23 (procuration of a girl under 21) of the Sexual Offences Act 1956;

(d) offences under Section 12(1) (taking a motor vehicle or other conveyance without authority, etc) or 25(1) (going equipped for stealing etc) of the Theft Act 1968;

(e) any offence under the Football (Offences) Act 1991;

(f) an offence under Section 2 Obscene Publications Act 1959 (publication of obscene matter);

(g) an offence under Section 1 Protection of Children Act 1978 (taking, distributing or showing indecent photographs or pseudo-photographs of children);

(h) an offence under Section 166 Criminal Justice and Public Order Act 1994 (sale of tickets at designated football match by a person not authorised to do so);

(i) an offence under Section 19 Public Order Act 1986 (publishing etc material intended or likely to stir up racial hatred);

(j) an offence under Section 167 Criminal Justice and Public Order Act 1994 (touting for car hire services);

(k) an offence under Section 11 Prevention of Crime Act 1953 (prohibition on carrying offensive weapons without lawful authority or reasonable excuse);

(l) an offence under Section 139(1) Criminal Justice Act 1988 (having an article with a blade or point in a public place);

(m) an offence under Section 139A(1) or (2) Criminal Justice Act 1988 (having an article with a blade or point or offensive weapon on school premises);

(n) an offence under Section 2 Protection from Harassment Act 1997 (harassment).

Ss (3)
Without prejudice to Section 2 of the Criminal Attempts Act 1981, the powers of summary arrest conferred by the following Sub-sections shall also apply to the offences of:

(a) conspiring to commit any of the offences mentioned in Sub-section (2) above;

(b) attempting to commit any such offence other than an offence under Section 12(1) of the Theft Act 1968;

(c) inciting, aiding, abetting, counselling or procuring the commission of any such offence;

and such offences are also arrestable offences for the purposes of this Act.

Ss (4)
Any person may arrest without a warrant:

(a) anyone who is in the act of committing an arrestable offence;

(b) anyone whom she or he has reasonable grounds for suspecting to be committing such an offence.

Ss (5)
When an arrestable offence has been committed, any person may arrest without a warrant:

(a) anyone who is guilty of the offence;

(b) anyone whom she or he has reasonable grounds for suspecting to be guilty of it.

Ss (6)
When a constable has reasonable grounds for suspecting that an arrestable offence has been committed, she or he may arrest without warrant anyone whom she or he has reasonable grounds for suspecting to be guilty of the offence.

Ss (7)
A constable may arrest without a warrant:

(a) anyone who is about to commit an arrestable offence;

(b) anyone whom she or he has reasonable grounds for suspecting to be about to commit an arrestable offence.

8.2. General power of arrest

Section 25 Police and Criminal Evidence Act 1984

Ss (1)
If a constable has reasonable grounds for suspecting that an offence which is not an **'arrestable offence'** has been committed or attempted – or is being committed or attempted – she or he may arrest the relevant person if it appears to her or him that service of a summons is impracticable or inappropriate because any of the general arrest conditions is satisfied.

Ss (2)
In this Section **'relevant person'** means any person whom the constable has reasonable grounds to suspect of having committed or having attempted to commit the offence – or of being in the course of committing or attempting to commit it.

Ss (3)
The general arrest conditions are:

(a) that the name of the relevant person is unknown to – and cannot be readily ascertained by – the constable;

(b) that the constable has reasonable grounds for doubting whether a name furnished by the relevant person as her or his name, actually is her or his real name;

(c) that –
  i. the relevant person has failed to furnish a **'satisfactory address'** for service (see Ss(4)), or
  ii. the constable has reasonable grounds to doubt that the address furnished by the relevant person is a satisfactory address for service;

(d) that the constable has reasonable grounds for believing that arrest is necessary to prevent the relevant person –
  i. causing physical injury to her or himself or any other person,
  ii. suffering physical injury,
  iii. causing loss of or damage to property,
  iv. committing an offence against public decency,
  v. causing unlawful obstruction of the highway;

(e) the constable has reasonable grounds for believing that arrest is necessary to protect a child or other vulnerable person – from the relevant person*.

* In respect of the general arrest condition shown at Paragraph (e) – if the child has been removed (for example, under the authority of police protection) and there are no other children involved, this condition may well be regarded as inappropriate since the child can no longer be considered at risk.

Ss (4)

For the purposes of Sub-section (3) above, an address is a **'satisfactory address'** for the service of a summons if it appears to the constable:

(a) that the relevant person will be at that address for a sufficiently long period for it to be possible to serve her or him with a summons; or

(b) that some other person specified by the relevant person will accept service of a summons for the relevant person at that address.

Ss (5)

Nothing in Sub-section 3(d) above authorises the arrest of a person under Sub-Paragraph (iv) (committing an offence against public decency) – except in cases when members of the public going about their normal business cannot reasonably be expected to avoid the person to be arrested.

8.3. Human rights implications for police powers of arrest

ECHR Article 5

ECHR Article 5 (Right to Liberty and Security) impacts on the use of police powers of arrest. Generally, Police and Criminal Evidence Act powers of arrest and Codes of Practice on detention comply broadly with ECHR principles provided the provisions of the Act and Codes are scrupulously followed. The impact of this is that police officers must be sure of their powers of arrest and use them correctly so that they are in a position to justify their use.

Agreeing with previous decided cases in the UK, the grounds for the arrest must be communicated to the arrested person as soon as possible. This should not be in technical or legal terms, but in everyday language.

Where police powers of stop/search and arrest subject to 'reasonable suspicion' are used, the 'objective observer' test should be employed. In terms of the ECHR principles of proportionality and necessity, it will also be necessary for police officers to justify the use of powers of arrest. Arrests should not be undertaken lightly or arbitrarily, each case should be considered on its own merits and officers should ask themselves if it is necessary to arrest in the specific circumstances. 'Positive arrest' policies may be held unlawful if challenged. (Also see Chapter 10.)

8.4. Repeal of statutory powers of arrest and preserved powers of arrest

Section 26 Police and Criminal Evidence Act 1984

Ss (1)

Subject to Sub-section (2) below, so much of any Act (including a local Act) – passed before the Police and Criminal Evidence Act – as enables a constable:

(a) to arrest a person for an offence without a warrant; or

(b) to arrest a person otherwise than for an offence without a warrant or an order of a court;

shall cease to have effect.

Ss (2)

Nothing in Sub-section (1) above affects the enactments specified in Schedule 2 of this Act (see Notes below).

Notes

This Section only refers to powers of arrest limited for use by the police and enshrined in legislation made prior to 1984. It does nor apply to powers of arrest available for the use of any person (ie breach of the peace).

The enactments specified in Schedule 2 of the Police and Criminal Evidence Act 1984 are:

Section 17(2) Military Lands Act 1892;
Section 12(1) Protection of Animals Act 1911;
Section 2 Emergency Powers Act 1920;
Section 7(3) Public Order Act 1936;
Section 49 Prison Act 1952;
Section 13 Visiting Forces Act 1952;
Sections 186 and 190B Army Act 1955;
Sections 186 and 190B Air Force Act 1955;
Section 104 and 105 Naval Discipline Act 1957;
Section 1(3) Street Offences Act 1959;
Section 32 Children and Young Persons Act 1969;
Section 24(2) Immigration Act 1971 and Paragraphs 17, 24 and 33 of Schedule 2 and Paragraph 7 of Schedule 3 to that Act;
Section 7 Bail Act 1976;
Sections 6(6), 7(11), 8(4), 9(7) and 10(5) Criminal Law Act 1977;
Schedule 5 Reserve Forces Act 1980;
Sections 60(5) and 61(1) Animal Health Act 1981;
Rule 36 in Schedule 1 Representation of the People Act 1983;
Sections 18, 35(10), 36(8), 38(7), 136(1) and 138 Mental Health Act 1983;
Section 5(5) Repatriation of Prisoners Act 1984.

8.5. Arrest of a child or young person absent from a place of safety without consent

If a child or young person is absent, without the consent of the responsible person:

a. from a place of safety to which she or he has been taken under Section 16(3) of this Act; or
b. from local authority accommodation -
   i. in which she or he is required to live under Section 12AA of this Act,
   ii. to which she or he has been remanded under Section 16(3A) of this Act, or
   iii. to which she or he has been remanded under Section 23(1) of this Act;

she or he may be arrested by a constable anywhere in the United Kingdom or Channel Islands without a warrant.

A person so arrested shall be conducted to:

a. the place of safety;
b. the local authority accommodation; or
c. such other place as the responsible person may direct, at the responsible person's expense.

Section 32(1A) and 1(B) Children and Young Persons Act 1969

Notes

'Responsible person' means the person who made the arrangements under Section 16(3) of the Act or the authority designated under Sections 12AA, 16(3B) or 23 of the Act.

Section 16(3) of the Act deals with arrangements made to detain a child or young person after she or he has been arrested on a warrant for being in breach of a supervision order.

Section 12AA of the Act deals with young offenders being required by the court to live in local authority accommodation.

Section 23(1) of the Act deals with children and young persons remanded into the care of a local authority for trial or sentence.

8.6. Cross-border arrests

Any constable - of a police force in England and Wales, or Scotland or Northern Ireland - who has reasonable grounds for suspecting that an offence has been committed or attempted in the country where his or her force is situated - and that the suspected person is in one of the other above-mentioned countries - may exercise in the relevant country the same powers of arrest and detention which it would be lawful to have exercised in the 'home' country.

Section 136 Criminal Justice and Public Order Act 1994

FIG 7: POWERS OF ARREST

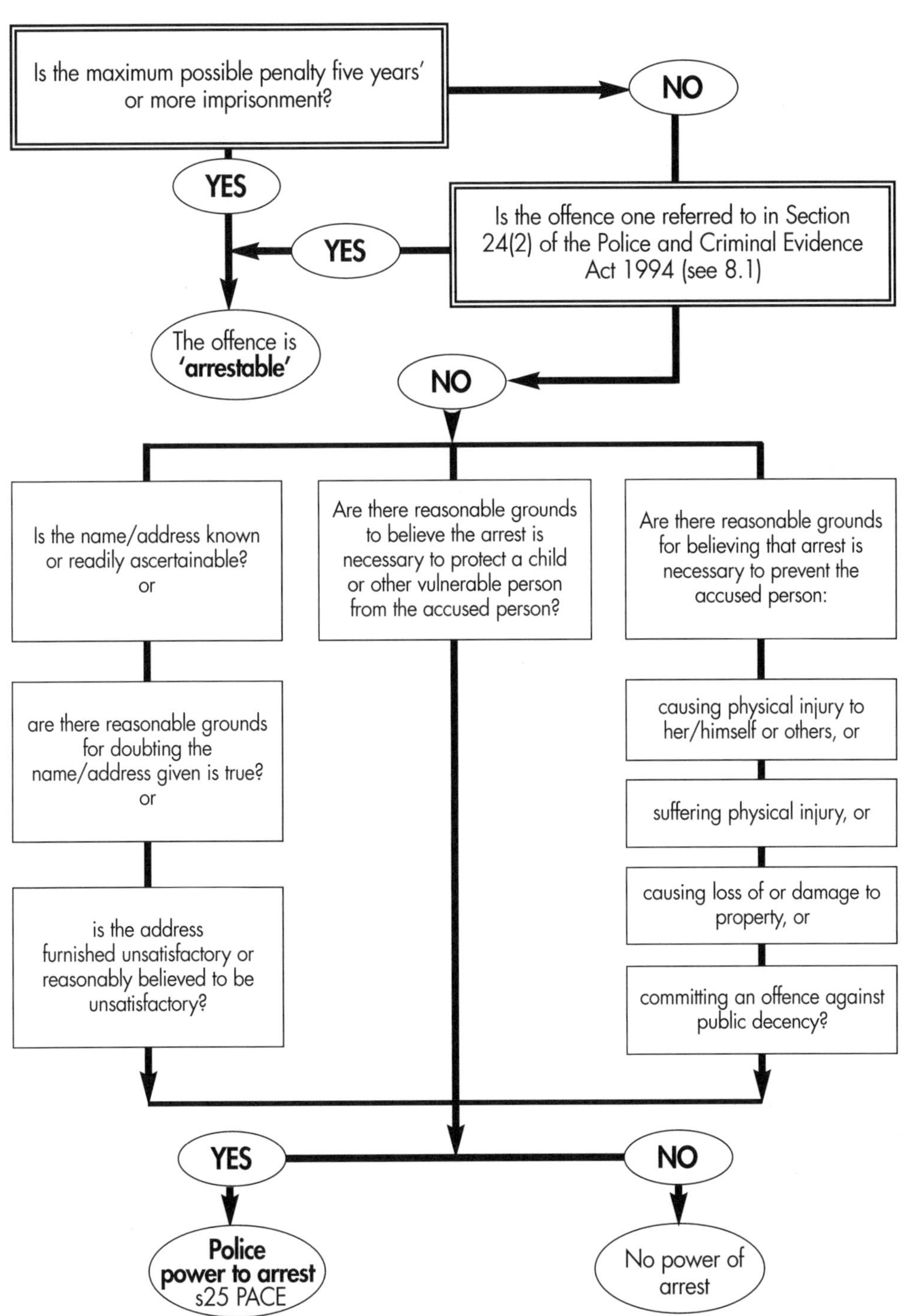

CHAPTER 9

POWERS TO SEARCH

9.1. Search, seizure and human rights

Article 8 and Protocol 1 (Article 1) ECHR

Police officers should be aware that use of search and seizure powers will infringe the rights of citizens. The rights are covered in ECHR Article 8 (Respect for Private and Family Life) and Protocol 1, Article 1, (Protection of Property). All such intrusions into family life must be capable of justification using the ECHR legal principles.

Courts will not accept that, because there is a statutory power of entry or seizure, it can be used without regard to the circumstances of the specific case.

Also, police officers should carefully consider the use of their powers when seizing property, as hasty or ill-considered use of powers may be challenged in the courts (also see Chapter 10).

9.2. Powers to search for a person without warrant

Section 17 Police and Criminal Evidence Act 1984

Ss (1)

Subject to the following provisions of this Section and without prejudice to any other enactment, a constable may enter and search any **'premises'** for the purpose:

(a) of executing -
   i. a warrant of arrest issued in connection with or arising out of criminal proceedings, or
   ii. a warrant of commitment issued under Section 76 Magistrates' Courts Act 1980;

(b) of arresting a person for an arrestable offence;

(c) of arresting a person for an offence under -
   i. Section 1 Public Order Act 1936 (prohibition of uniforms in connection with political objects),
   ii. any enactment contained in Sections 6 to 8 or 10 Criminal Law Act 1977 (offences relating to entering and remaining on property),
   iii. Section 4 Public Order Act 1986 (fear or provocation of violence),
   iv. Section 76 Criminal Justice and Public Order Act 1994 (failure to comply with an interim possession order);

(ca) of arresting, in pursuance of Section 32(1A) Children and Young Persons Act 1969, any child who has been remanded or committed to local authority accommodation under Section 23(1) of that Act;

(cb) of recapturing any person who is or is deemed for any purpose to be unlawfully at large while liable to be detained -
   i. in a prison, remand centre, young offender institution or secure training centre, or
   ii. in pursuance of Section 53 Children and Young Persons Act 1933 (dealing with children and young persons guilty of grave crimes), in any other place;

(d) of recapturing any person whatever who is unlawfully at large and whom the constable is pursuing; or

(e) of saving life and limb or to prevent serious damage to property.

Notes

'Premises' includes vehicles and tents (Section 23 Police and Criminal Evidence Act 1984).

In this Section police officers may use reasonable force to effect an entry (Section 117 Police and Criminal Evidence Act 1984).

To effect an entry under this Section, **'reasonable grounds'** are required in respect of all the circumstances shown above with the exception of those shown at Ss (1)(e). A constable only requires **'grounds'** to enter in the case of Paragraph (e). In the circumstances set out in Paragraph (e) the officer only requires grounds for believing life and limb are at risk or that it is necessary for the prevention of serious damage to property. Grounds are of a lower standard of suspicion than reasonable grounds (Section 17(2) Police and Criminal Evidence Act 1984).

In respect of all the circumstances shown above - with the exception of those shown at (e) - if the premises consist of two or more separate dwellings, the power of search is limited to the parts of the premises that are used in common between the occupants of the dwelling to be searched and the occupants of any other dwelling - and any dwelling that the police have reasonable grounds to suspect the person they are looking for to be in (Section 17(2) Police and Criminal Evidence Act 1984).

The power of search in this Section may only be exercised by a constable in uniform when used for the purposes specified in Sub-section (1)(c) (ii) or (iv), (Section 17(3) Police and Criminal Evidence Act 1984).

The power conferred by this Section is only a power to search to the extent that is reasonably required for the purpose for which the power of entry is used, (Section 17(4) PACE).

9.3. Powers to search for a person with a warrant

9.3a. Powers to assist in the discovery of children who may be in need of emergency protection

Section 48 Children Act 1989

Ss (1)

When it appears to a court making an emergency protection order that adequate information as to the child's whereabouts:

(a) is not available to the applicant for the order; but

(b) is available to another person;

it may include in the order a provision requiring that other person to disclose - if asked to do so by the applicant - any information that she or he may have as to the child's whereabouts.

Ss (2)

No person shall be excused from complying with such a requirement on the ground that complying might incriminate her or him or her or his spouse of an offence - though a statement or admission made in complying shall not be admissible in evidence against either of them in proceedings for any offence other than perjury.

Ss (3)

An emergency protection order may authorise the applicant to enter premises specified by the order and search for the child with respect to whom the order is made.

Ss (4)

If the court is satisfied that there is reasonable cause to believe that there may be another child on those premises with respect to whom an emergency protection order ought to be made, it may make an order authorising the applicant to search for that other child on those premises.

Ss (5)

In cases in which;

(a) an order has been made under Sub-section (4) above;

(b) the child concerned has been found on the premises; and

(c) the applicant is satisfied that the grounds for making an emergency protection order exist with respect to her or him;

the order shall have effect as if it were an emergency protection order.

Ss (6)

When an order has been made under Sub-section (4), the applicant shall notify the court of its effect.

Ss (7)
A person shall be guilty of an offence if she or he intentionally obstructs any person exercising the power of entry and search under Sub-sections (3) or (4).

Ss (8)
A person guilty of an offence under Sub-section (7) shall be liable on summary conviction to a fine not exceeding level 3 (£1,000 at the time of going to press) on the standard scale.

Ss (9)
If, on an application made by any person for a warrant under this Section, it appears to the court:

(a) that a person attempting to exercise powers under an emergency protection order has been prevented from doing so by being refused entry to the premises concerned, or access to the child concerned; or

(b) that any such person is likely to be prevented from exercising any such powers; it may issue a warrant authorising any constable to assist the person - mentioned in Paragraphs (a) or (b) of this Sub-section - in the exercise of those powers, using reasonable force if necessary.

Ss (10)
Every warrant issued under this Section shall be addressed to, and executed by, a constable who shall be accompanied by the person applying for the warrant if:

(a) that person so desires; and

(b) the court by whom the warrant is issued does not direct otherwise.

Ss (11)
A court granting an application for a warrant under this Section may direct that the constable concerned may, in executing the warrant, be accompanied by a registered medical practitioner, registered nurse or registered health visitor if she or he so chooses.

Ss (12)
An application for a warrant under this Section shall be made in the manner and form prescribed by the rules of court.

Ss (13)
Whenever it is reasonably practicable to do so, an Order under Sub-section (4) (previous page), an application for a warrant under this Section and any such warrant shall name the child - and if it does not name her or him it shall describe her or him as clearly as possible.

9.3b.Recovery of abducted children etc

Section 50 Children Act 1989

Ss (1)
If it appears to the court that there is reason to believe that a child to whom this Section applies:

(a) has been unlawfully taken away or is being unlawfully kept away from the responsible person;

(b) has run away or is staying away from the responsible person; or

(c) is missing;

the court may make an order under this Section - a **'recovery order'** (see Sss (3) to (5) below).

Ss (2)
This Section applies in relation to a child who is:

(a) in care;

(b) the subject of an emergency protection order; or

(c) in police protection;

and in this Section the **'responsible person'** means any person who for the time being has care of her or him - by virtue of the care order, the emergency protection order, or police protection, as the case may be.

Ss (3)
A **'recovery order'**:

(a) operates as a direction to any person, who is in a position to do so, to produce the child on request to any **'authorised person'** (see Ss (7) overleaf);

(b) authorises the removal of the child by any authorised person;

(c) requires any person who has information as to the child's whereabouts to disclose that information, if asked to do so, to a constable or an officer of the court; and

(d) authorises a constable to enter any **'premises'** specified in the order and search for the child - using **'reasonable force'** if necessary (see Ss (6) below).

Ss (4)

The court may make a **'recovery order'** only on the application of:

(a) any person who has parental responsibility for the child by virtue of a care order or emergency protection order; or

(b) if the child is in police protection, the designated officer.

Ss (5)

A **'recovery order'** shall name the child and:

(a) any person who has parental responsibility for the child, by virtue of a care order or emergency protection order; or

(b) if the child is in police protection, the designated officer.

Ss (6)

'Premises' may only be specified under Sub-section (3)(d) if it appears to the court that there are reasonable grounds for believing the child to be on them.

Ss (7)

In this Section an **'authorised person'** means:

(a) any person specified by the court;

(b) any constable; and

(c) any person who is **'authorised'** (see Ss (8)) -
  i. after the recovery order is made; and
  ii. by a person who has parental responsibility for the child - by virtue of a care order or an emergency protection order - to exercise any power under a recovery order; and

the **'designated officer'** means the officer designated for the purposes of Section 46 (police protection).

Ss (8)

When a person is **'authorised'** as mentioned in Sub-section (7)(c):

(a) the authorisation shall identify the recovery order; and

(b) any person claiming to be so authorised shall, if asked to do so, produce some duly authenticated document showing that she or he is so authorised.

Ss (9)

A person shall be guilty of an offence if she or he intentionally obstructs an authorised person exercising the power under Sub-section (3)(b) to remove a child.

Ss (10)

A person guilty of an offence under this Section shall be liable on summary conviction to a fine not exceeding level 3 (£1,000 at the time of going to press) on the standard scale.

Ss (11)

No person shall be excused from complying with any request made under Sub-section (3)(c) on the ground that complying with it might incriminate her or him, or her or his spouse, of an offence - though a statement or admission made in complying shall not be admissible in evidence against either of them in proceedings for an offence other than perjury.

Ss (12)

If a child is made the subject of a recovery order while being looked after by a local authority, any reasonable expenses incurred by an authorised person in giving effect to the order shall be recoverable from the authority.

Ss (13)

A recovery order shall have effect in Scotland as if it had been made by the Court of Session and as if that court had had jurisdiction to make it.

9.4. Powers to search for property/evidence without warrant

9.4a. Search of premises where a person is arrested

> When a person has been arrested, a constable may enter and search any premises in which that person was arrested - or was immediately before her or his arrest - for evidence relating to the offence for which she or he was arrested - provided that the constable has reasonable grounds for believing that such evidence is on the premises.
>
> Section 32(2)(b) and 32(6) Police and Criminal Evidence Act 1984

9.4b. Search of premises occupied or controlled by a person arrested for an arrestable offence

Section 18 Police and Criminal Evidence Act 1984

Ss (1)
Subject to the following provisions of this Section, a constable may enter and search any premises - occupied or controlled by a person who is under arrest for an arrestable offence - if she or he has reasonable grounds for suspecting that, on the premises, there is evidence - other than items subject to legal privilege - that relates:

(a) to that offence; or

(b) to some other arrestable offence which is connected with or similar to that offence.

Ss (2)
A constable may seize and retain anything for which she or he may search under Sub-section (1) above.

Ss (3)
The power to search conferred by Sub-section (1) is only a power to search to the extent that is reasonably required for the purpose of discovering such evidence.

Ss (4)
Subject to Sub-section (5), the powers conferred by this Section may not be exercised unless an officer of the rank of Inspector or above has authorised them in writing.

Ss (5)
A constable may conduct a search under Sub-section (1):

(a) before taking the person to a police station; and

(b) without obtaining an authorisation under Sub-section (4);

if the presence of that person at a place other than a police station is necessary for the effective investigation of the offence.

Ss (6)
If a constable conducts a search by virtue of Sub-section (5), she or he shall inform an officer of the rank of Inspector or above that she or he has made the search as soon as practicable after she or he made it.

Ss (7)
An officer who:

(a) authorises a search; or

(b) is informed of a search under Sub-section (6) above, shall make a record in writing -
   i. of the grounds for the search, and
   ii. of the nature of the evidence sought.

Ss (8)
If the person - who was in occupation or control of the premises at the time of the search - is in police detention at the time the record is to be made, the officer shall make a record as part of her or his custody record.

Note

'Arrestable offence' is defined with reference to Section 24 Police and Criminal Evidence Act 1984 (see 8,1), (Section 118 Police and Criminal Evidence Act 1984).

9.5. Powers to search for property/evidence with warrant

9.5a. Search of premises for evidence of a serious arrestable offence

Section 8 Police and Criminal Evidence Act 1984

Ss (1)

If, on an application made by a constable, a Justice of the Peace is satisfied that there are reasonable grounds for believing:

(a) that a **'serious arrestable offence'** has been committed;

(b) that there is material on premises specified in the application which is likely to be of substantial value (whether by itself or together with other material) to the investigation of the offence;

(c) that the material is likely to be **'relevant evidence'**;

(d) that it does not consist of or include items subject to **'legal privilege', 'excluded material' or 'special procedure material'**; and

(e) that any of the conditions specified in Sub-section (3) below applies;

she or he may issue a warrant authorising a constable to enter and search the premises.

Ss (2)

A constable may seize or retain anything for which a search has been authorised under Ss (1) above.

Ss (3)

The conditions mentioned in Sub-section (1)(e) above are:

(a) that it is not practicable to communicate with any person entitled to grant entry to the premises; or

(b) that it is practicable to communicate with a person entitled to grant entry to the premises but it is not practicable to communicate with any person entitled to grant access to the evidence; and

(c) that entry to the premises will not be granted unless a warrant is produced; or

(d) that the purpose of a search may be frustrated or seriously prejudiced unless a constable arriving at the premises can secure immediate entry to them.

Ss (4)

In this Act **'relevant evidence'**, in relation to an offence, means anything that would be admissible in evidence at a trial for the offence.

Ss (5)

The power to issue a warrant conferred by this Section is in addition to any such power otherwise conferred.

Notes

This power gives police officers authority to search for evidence as opposed to specified articles ie, firearms or stolen goods. It could, therefore, be used to search for evidence of, for example, sexual abuse.

'Serious arrestable offence' includes;

1. Treason;
2. Murder;
3. Manslaughter;
4. Rape;
5. Kidnapping;
6. Incest With a Girl Under 13 Years of Age;
7. Buggery With a Person Under 16 Years of Age;
8. Indecent Assault Which Constitutes an Act of Gross Indecency;
9. Causing an Explosion Likely to Endanger Life or Property (Section 2 Explosive Substances Act 1883);
10. Intercourse With a Girl Under 13 Years of Age (Section 5 Sexual Offences Act 1956);
11. Possessing Firearms With Intent to Injure (Section 16 Firearms Act 1968);
12. Use of Firearms or Imitation Firearms with Intent to Resist Arrest (Section 17(1) Firearms Act 1968);
13. Carrying Firearms With Criminal Intent (Section 18 Firearms Act 1968);

14. Hostage Taking (Section 1 Taking of Hostages Act 1982);
15. Hi-jacking (Section 1, Aviation Security Act 1982);
16. Torture (Section 134 Criminal Justice Act 1988);
17. Causing Death by Dangerous Driving (Section 1 Road Traffic Act 1988);
18. Causing Death by Careless Driving When Under the Influence of Drink or Drugs (Section 3A Road Traffic Act 1988);
19. Endangering Safety at Aerodromes (Section 1 Aviation and Maritime Security Act 1990);
20. Hi-jacking Ships (Section 9 Aviation and Maritime Security Act 1990);
21. Seizing or Exercising Control of Fixed Platforms (Section 10 Aviation and Maritime Security Act 1990);
22. Indecent Photographs and Pseudo-photographs of Children (Section 1 Protection of Children Act 1978);
23. Publication of Obscene Matter (Section 2 Obscene Publications Act 1959): and
24. any offence mentioned in Paragraphs (a) to (f) of Section 1(3) Drug Trafficking Act 1994;

(Schedule 5 Police and Criminal Evidence Act 1984).

...Also any other arrestable offence which has led to or is intended or likely to lead to:

(a) serious harm to the security of the State or to public order;
(b) serious interference with the administration of justice or with the investigation of offences or a particular offence;
(c) the death of any person;
(d) serious injury to any person;
(e) substantial financial gain to any person; and
(f) serious financial loss to any person.

'Loss' is serious for these purposes if, having regard to all the circumstances, it is serious for the person who suffers it. For these purposes, **'injury'** includes any disease and any impairment of a person's physical or mental condition.

(Section 116(3), (6), (7) and (8) Police and Criminal Evidence Act 1984.)

'Legal privilege', 'excluded material' and 'special procedural material' are basically confidential items of material that are held in confidence by a professional person, her or his client, or a go-between. Items subject to legal privilege can never be searched for, but excluded and special procedural material can be obtained in certain circumstances. See Sections 9 to 14 and Schedule 2 of the Police and Criminal Evidence Act 1984 for further information AND seek advice should you become involved with this material.

It is also worth noting that you may enter and search premises with a warrant under this Section to photograph evidence - for example, living conditions - by virtue of the Codes of Practice to the Police and Criminal Evidence Act 1984, Code B, Paragraph 6.4.

9.6. Powers to seize evidence when lawfully on premises

Section 19 Police and Criminal Evidence Act 1984

Ss (1)

The powers conferred by Sub-sections (2), (3) and (4) below are exercisable by a constable who is lawfully on any premises.

Ss (2)

The constable may seize anything which is on the premises if she or he has reasonable grounds for believing that:

(a) it has been obtained in consequence of the commission of an offence; AND

(b) it is necessary to seize it, to prevent it being concealed, lost, damaged, altered or destroyed.

Ss (3)

The constable may seize anything which is on the premises if she or he has reasonable grounds for believing:

(a) that it is evidence in relation to an offence which she or he is investigating, or any other offence; AND

(b) that it is necessary to seize it, to prevent the evidence being concealed, lost, altered or destroyed.

Ss (4)

The constable may require any information which is contained in a computer and is accessible from the premises - to be produced in a form in which it can be taken away and in which it is visible and legible - if she or he has reasonable grounds for believing:

(a) that -
   i. it is evidence in relation to an offence which she or he is investigating, or any other offence, or
   ii. it has been obtained in consequence of the commission of an offence; and

(b) that it is necessary to do so in order to prevent it being concealed, lost, tampered with or destroyed.

Ss (5)

The powers conferred by this Section are in addition to any power otherwise conferred.

Ss (6)

No power of seizure conferred on a constable under any enactment (including an enactment contained in an Act passed after this Act) is to be taken to authorise the seizure of an item which the constable exercising the power has reasonable grounds for believing to be subject to legal privilege.

FIG 8: POWERS TO SEARCH

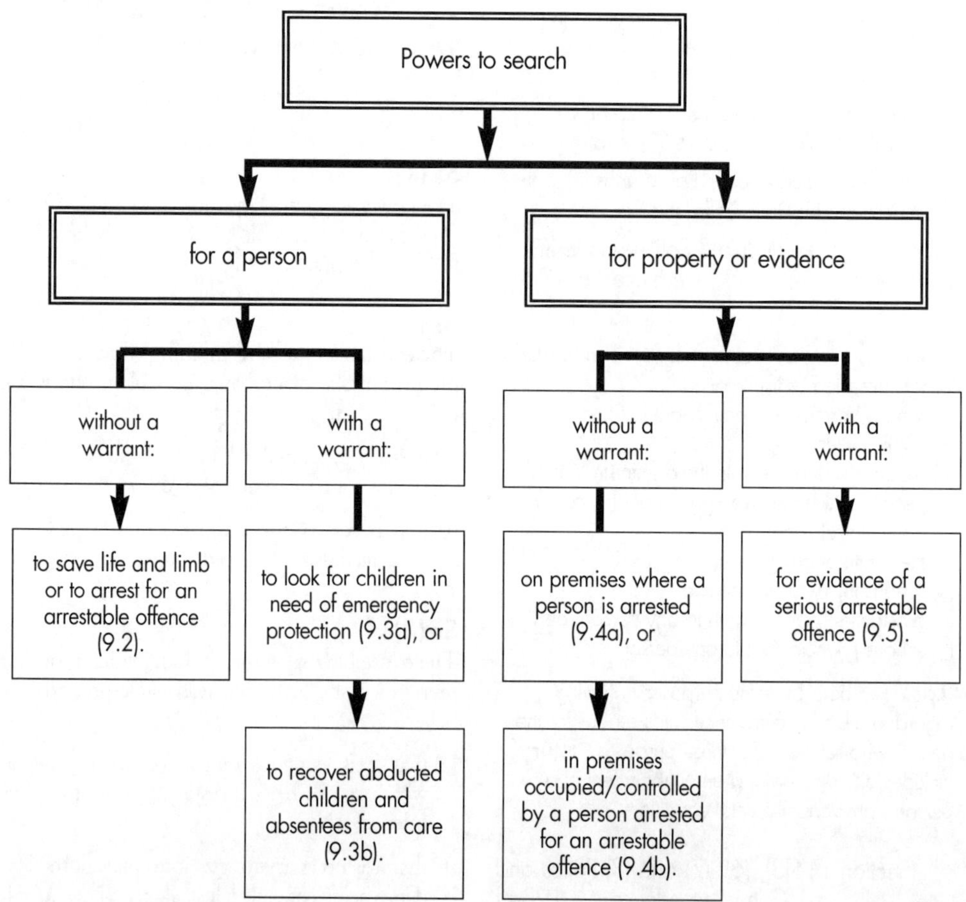

CHAPTER 10

HUMAN RIGHTS

10.1. Will human rights legislation affect operational policing?

Many people have asked how human rights legislation will affect operational policing and support functions. The answer to this is easy.

> Every time a police officer or member of police support staff makes a decision, a person's rights may be affected, therefore that is how operational policing will be affected.
>
> Every time a police officer uses bodily force, a power of arrest, search, seizure or uses surveillance or interrogation methods, another person's rights are affected. The police officer must therefore consider the use of that power and may have to justify its use in any subsequent legal proceedings.
>
> Every time a support staff member responds to enquiries or requests for assistance by telephone, at the front counter or by other means of communication, they may infringe another person's human rights, therefore they need to consider the provisions of the Human Rights Act.

The reader can begin to see that the Human Rights Act will have a tremendous impact on operational policing and support functions. We must then add the fact that police officers now have a duty to positively uphold and protect the human rights of citizens.

Specifically, police officers have a duty to take measures to protect life, including a duty to put in place effective criminal law provisions to deter the commission of offences against the person, backed up by law enforcement machinery for the prevention, suppression and sanctioning of breaches for such provisions.

Consequently, there is a greater emphasis on the prevention and protection role and responsibility of police officers. This is especially so in relation to child victims. Child Protection has therefore assumed an even higher importance in the police response to prevent and detect crime.

10.2. Human Rights Act 1998

The main objective of the Human Rights Act was to incorporate human rights law into the legal system of the United Kingdom. This was implemented by adopting certain Articles of the European Convention on Human Rights (ECHR). In this book we will only be looking at the aspects of human rights law which directly affect child protection issues. (For more information on this subject, see the further reading list at the end of the book.)

The Articles we will cover in this chapter are:

Article 2	Right to Life
Article 5	Right to Liberty and Security
Article 6	Right to a Fair Trial
Article 8	Right to Private and Family Life
Article 12	Right to Marry
Protocol 1, Article 1	Protection of Property
Protocol 1, Article 2:	Right to Education

10.2a. General principles under the Human Rights Act 1998

- Definition of 'public authority'
- Definition of 'victim'
- Definition of 'Proportionality'.

10.2a.i. Definition of 'public authority'

Section 6 Human Rights Act 1998

Ss (1)
It is unlawful for a public authority to act in a way which is incompatible with a Convention right.

Ss(2)
Subsection (1) does not apply to an act if:

(a) as the result of one or more provisions of primary legislation, the authority could not have acted differently; or

(b) in the case of one or more provisions of or made under primary legislation, which cannot be read or given effect in a way compatible with the Convention rights, the authority was acting so as to give effect to or enforce those provisions.

Ss (3)
In this section 'public authority' includes:

(a) a court or tribunal;

(b) any person having certain functions of a public nature - but does not include either House of Parliament or a person exercising functions in connection with proceedings in Parliament.

Ss (4)
In subsection (3) 'Parliament' does not include the House of Lords in its judicial capacity.

Ss (5)
In relation to a particular act, a person is not a public authority by virtue only of subsection (3)(b) if the nature of the act is private.

Ss (6)
An 'act' includes a failure to act but does not include a failure to:

(a) introduce in or lay before Parliament a proposal for legislation; or

(b) make any primary legislation or remedial order.

Note

Clearly, police officers are covered by the Human Rights Act as defined in Section 6(3). It should be noted however, that other organisations involved in Child Protection functions will also be 'public authorities' as defined. Therefore all the principles mentioned above in relation to protection of children's rights also apply to partner organisations, who share responsibility with the police.

10.2a.ii. Definition of 'victim'

The definition of a 'victim', as a person who can bring an action under Section 7 of the Human Rights Act, is quite tight. It has been built up over the years from decided cases and Article 34 of the Convention.

Victims can be legal or natural persons, non-government organisations and corporate bodies.

Only persons who are 'directly affected' or at risk of being affected by an act or omission can claim to be victims. Public authorities cannot claim to be victims.

Notes

It is important that police officers understand the definition of a victim and, in line with their duty, recognise and uphold their rights.

10.2a.iii. Definition of 'proportionality'

Proportionality means that 'there must be a reasonable relationship between the aim to be achieved and the means used'.

Proportionality requires public authorities to take only such measures that are strictly necessary to achieve the required objective. The least intrusive methods of operating should be used. The saying 'Don't use a sledgehammer to crack a nut' applies in practice.

Notes

When applying the proportionality test, police officers and support staff must take account of the rights of the individual and others who may be affected, such as family members and business colleagues.

10.3. European Convention on Human Rights (ECHR) - overview

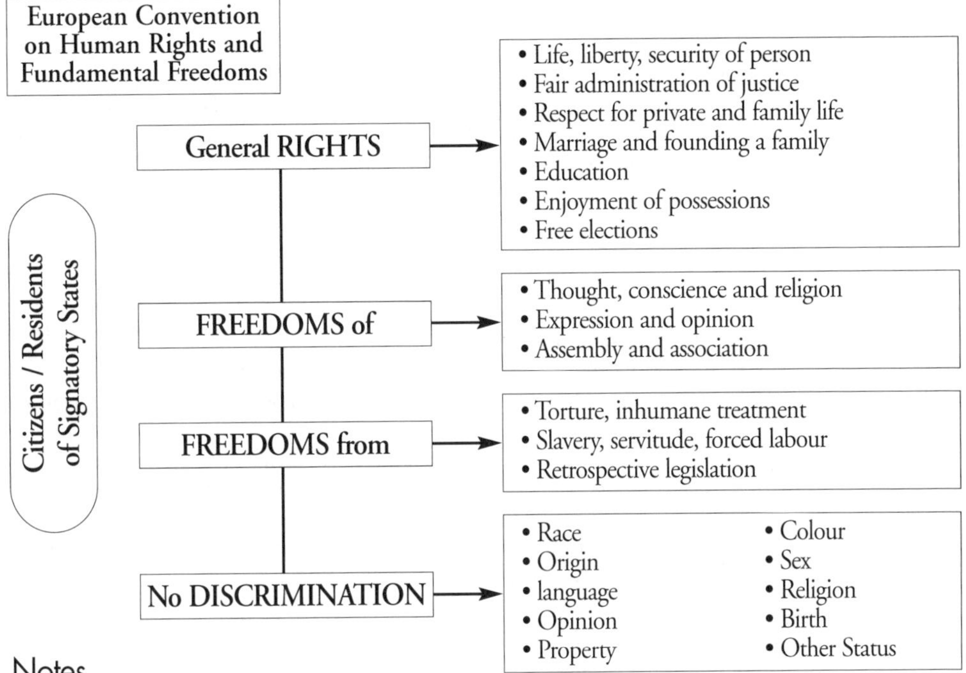

Notes

The rights of UK citizens are now written in the *Bill of Rights* of ECHR which may make them more certain and more widely understood. (The rights provided by ECHR should, however, be regarded as a minimum standard and recent UK legislation generally offers a higher standard of rights.)

It is important to realise that the law demands that the police have a positive duty to protect and enforce individual citizen's human rights.

10.4. Articles relevant to child protection

Summary of Articles relevant to child protection

Article 2	Right to Life
Article 5	Right to Liberty and Security
Article 6	Right to a Fair Trial
Article 8	Right to Respect for Private and Family Life
Article 12	Right to Marry
Protocol 1, Article 1	Protection of Property
Protocol 1, Article 2	Right to Education

10.4a. Right to life

Article 2, ECHR

Paragraph 1

Everyone's right to life shall be protected by law. No one shall be deprived of his life intentionally, (save in the execution of a sentence of a court following his conviction of a crime for which this penalty is provided by law).

(Note however that ECHR Protocol 6 (Article 3) abolishes the death penalty.)

Paragraph 2

Deprivation of life shall not be regarded as inflicted in contravention of this Article when it results from the use of force which is no more than absolutely necessary:

(a) in defence of any person from unlawful violence;

(b) in order to effect a lawful arrest or to prevent the escape of a person lawfully detained;

(c) in action lawfully taken for the purpose of quelling a riot or insurrection.

Operational policing areas covered by Article 2

- Arrest
- Use of force - lethal/non-lethal
- Treatment of prisoners
- Handcuffing

10.4b. Right to liberty and security

Article 5, ECHR

Paragraph 1

Everyone has the right to liberty and security of person. No one shall be deprived of his liberty - save in the following cases and in accordance with a procedure prescribed by law:

(a) the lawful detention of a person after conviction by a competent court;

(b) the lawful arrest or detention of a person for non-compliance with the lawful order of a court or in order to secure the fulfilment of any obligation prescribed by law;

(c) the lawful arrest or detention of a person effected for the purpose of bringing him before the competent legal authority - on reasonable suspicion of having committed an offence, or when it is reasonably considered necessary to prevent his committing an offence, or fleeing after having done so;

(d) the detention of a minor by lawful order for the purpose of educational supervision or his lawful detention for the purpose of bringing him before the competent legal authority;

(e) The lawful detention of persons for the prevention of the spreading of infectious diseases, of persons of unsound mind, alcoholics or drug addicts or vagrants;

(f) The lawful arrest or detention of a person to prevent his effecting an unauthorised entry into the country or of a person against whom action is being taken with a view to deportation or extradition.

Paragraph 2

Everyone who is arrested shall be informed promptly, in a language which he understands, of the reasons for his arrest and of any charge against him.

Paragraph 3

Everyone arrested or detained in accordance with the provisions of Paragraph 1(c) of this Article shall be brought promptly before a judge or other officer authorised by law to exercise judicial power and shall be entitled to trial within a reasonable time or to release pending trial. Release may be conditioned by guarantees to appear for trial.

Paragraph 4

Everyone who is deprived of his liberty by arrest or detention shall be entitled to take proceedings by which the lawfulness of his detention shall be decided speedily by a court and his release ordered if the detention is not lawful.

Paragraph 5

Everyone who has been the victim of arrest or detention in contravention of the provisions of this Article shall have an enforceable right to compensation.

Notes

This Article impacts heavily on operational policing in many areas. Generally, Police and Criminal Evidence Act powers of arrest, and Codes of Practice on detention, comply broadly with ECHR principles *provided* the provisions of the Act and Codes are scrupulously followed.

The impact of this is that police officers must be sure of their powers of arrest and use them correctly so that they are in a position to justify their use.

Agreeing with previous decided cases in the UK, the grounds for the arrest must be communicated to the arrested person as soon as possible. This should not be in technical or legal terms, but in everyday language.

Where police powers of stop/search and arrest subject to 'reasonable suspicion' are used, the '**objective observer**' test should be employed. In practice this means that the arresting/searching officer must be able to clearly relate the grounds of his/her suspicion to an objective bystander. If the bystander would accept and endorse the reasons for the officer's suspicion then the arrest or search would be lawful. This situation is no different to good practice that existed prior to the commencement of the Human Rights Act.

In terms of the ECHR principles of proportionality and necessity, it will also be necessary for police officers to justify the use of powers of arrest. Arrests should not be undertaken lightly or arbitrarily. Each case should be considered on its own merits and officers should ask themselves if it is necessary to arrest in the specific circumstances. 'Positive arrest' policies may be held unlawful if challenged.

10.4c. Right to a fair trial

Article 6, ECHR

Paragraph 1

In the determination of his civil rights and obligations, or of any criminal charge against him, every person is entitled to a fair and public hearing, within a reasonable time, by an independent and impartial tribunal established by law.

Judgment shall be pronounced publicly, but the press and public may be excluded from all or part of the trial:

- in the interests of morals, public order or national security in a democratic society;
- where the interests of juveniles or the protection of the private life of the parties so require; or,
- to the extent strictly necessary in the opinion of the court in special circumstances where publicity would prejudice the interests of justice.

Paragraph 2

Everyone charged with a criminal offence shall be presumed innocent until proved guilty according to law.

Paragraph 3

Everyone charged with a criminal offence has the following minimum rights:

(a) to be informed promptly, in a language which he understands and in detail, of the nature and cause of the accusation against him;

(b) to have adequate time and facilities for the preparation of his defence;

(c) to defend himself in person or through legal assistance of his own choosing or, if he has not sufficient means to pay for legal assistance, to be given legal assistance free of charge when the interests of justice so require;

(d) to examine or have examined witnesses against him, and to obtain the attendance and examination of witnesses on his behalf under the same conditions as witnesses against him;

(e) to have the free assistance of an interpreter if he cannot understand or speak the language used in court.

Notes

Police officers should be aware that ECHR provides extra guarantees in criminal cases:

- the right to be informed promptly of the accusation
- adequate time to prepare a defence
- the right to defend in person
- the right to examine witnesses in person
- the right to an interpreter.

There have been recent developments in the trial of juveniles in adult courts to ensure fairness and compliance with the rules of natural justice.

The principle of 'equality of arms' means that the defence in a case should have access to the same level of information as the prosecution, including 'unused material'.

Accused's right to cross-examine. To ensure the right to a fair trial, Article 6 sets many criteria, one of which is that the defendant has the right to defend him/herself in person (Article 6(3)c)).

In the UK in recent years, several cases involving serious sexual assaults have been brought to trial in which the defendant represented himself and which resulted in undue stress, embarrassment, harassment and humiliation to the victim by means of the detailed questioning of her by the defendant. The female victims were unfairly subjected to lengthy periods of cross-examination about their personal lives and sexual habits. As a result of these experiences, the Youth Justice and Criminal Evidence Act 1999 brought in restrictions prohibiting the right of unrepresented defendants to cross-examine witnesses in sexual offence cases. Also, the right to hear evidence of the sexual history of witnesses was curtailed with specific conditions, the main one being that such evidence could not be heard without leave of the court.

On the face of it, the 1999 Act is non-compliant with ECHR principles, and non-compliant with a decided case which held that the accused should be given an adequate and proper opportunity to challenge and question a witness against him/her. However, it has been held in other cases (in different circumstances), that the right to defend oneself under Article 6(3)c is not absolute, therefore we shall have to wait to see if this law is challenged before certainty can be established.

10.4d. Right to respect for private and family life

Article 8, ECHR

Paragraph 1

Everyone has the right to respect for his private and family life, his home and his correspondence.

Paragraph 2

There shall be no interference by a public authority with the exercise of this right - except such as is in accordance with the law and is necessary in a democratic society in the interests of national security, public safety or the economic well-being of the country, for the prevention of disorder or crime, for the protection of health or morals, or for the protection of the rights and freedoms of others.

Notes

This is a wide-ranging Article that safeguards personal privacy, family privacy and personal integrity. It therefore links to other Articles such as Article 5. As with all qualified rights, public authorities can breach an individual's rights but the infringement must be justified by the normal ECHR legal principles of legality, proportionality and necessity, and there also must be a justifiable 'legitimate aim' from the list provided within the Article.

Search/seizure. Where search warrants or powers of seizure of evidence are used, police officers must consider the rights to respect for private and family life and the privacy of correspondence.

All such intrusions into family life must be capable of justification using the ECHR legal principles. Courts will not accept that, because there is a statutory power of entry or seizure, it can be used without regard to the circumstances of the specific case. Each occasion an intrusive power is used it must be considered and justified on its own merits. On a practical note, police officers may find that courts and magistrates who are asked to grant warrants will scrutinise applications to a greater degree.

This Article will also have impacts on policing operations relating to trespassing and use of powers against Travellers or 'squatters', including the children involved.

Private life. The notion of 'private life' is a wide one and includes not only close family, but also the right to develop one's own personality and to create and foster relationships with others.

Also, if the police circulate information about prolific offenders (for example paedophiles) and place it in the public domain, there is an infringement of the alleged criminals' rights. A fair balance must be struck between the general interests of the community and the interests of individuals. Clear protocols now exist for exchange of information on convicted paedophiles and the requirement for registration of domicile with local police.

Protection of physical integrity. In the Osman case, police were warned about strange and threatening activities of an individual and they took no action. The court held that there was a positive duty for the police to protect the public as they had been negligent in failing to prevent two murders.

Positive obligations and policing

A duty to:

- safeguard the life and physical integrity of individuals known to be at risk
- investigate crime efficiently
- ensure that individuals can enjoy their own Convention rights

10.4e. Right to marry

Article 12, ECHR

Men and women of marriageable age have the right to marry and to found a family, according to the national laws governing the exercise of this right.

Notes

The national laws in the UK do not recognise the lawfulness of 'gay' marriages. Police officers may also deal with incidents relating to forceful abduction of women for the purposes of marriage and arranged marriages. These should be dealt with using the relevant legislation (see Chapter 3: Offences Involving Indecency).

10.4f. Protection of property

Protocol 1, Article 1, ECHR

Every natural or legal person is entitled to the peaceful enjoyment of his possessions. No one shall be deprived of his possessions except in the public interest and subject to the conditions provided for by law and by the general principles of international law.

The preceding provisions shall not, however, in any way impair the right of a State to enforce such laws as it deems necessary to control the use of property in accordance with the general interest, or to secure the payment of taxes or other contributions or penalties.

Notes

Police officers should carefully consider the use of their powers when seizing property, as hasty or ill-considered use of powers may be challenged in the courts. All seizures of property for evidential purposes should be justifiable and preferably provided for by a statutory power of seizure.

10.4g. Right to education

Protocol 1, Article 2, ECHR

No person shall be denied the right to education. In the exercise of any functions which it assumes in relation to education and to teaching, the State shall respect the right of parents to ensure such education and teaching in conformity with their own religious and philosophical convictions.

Notes

The UK has announced a reservation applicable to Protocol 1, Article 2. The general right of the Article 'is accepted by the UK only in so far as it is compatible with the provision of efficient instruction and training, and the avoidance of unreasonable public expenditure.' In other words, everyone has the right to education provided it can be delivered in a cost-effective manner.

Corporal punishment and 'parental chastisement'. All forms of corporal punishment are banned in local authority, special and grant-maintained schools in the UK.

Historically, there was a defence in UK common law of 'parental chastisement' against a charge of assault in which a parent had smacked their child. This defence allowed a parent to cause reasonable pain and discomfort to a child during the chastisement but not 'actual bodily harm' such as bruises or cuts. The UK common law defence allowed parents to inflict 'moderate and reasonable' chastisement on their children. When reviewing a case, the European Court of Human Rights held that the defence of lawful chastisement was too wide and failed to protect children adequately; and that it should therefore be amended.

The European Court has also heard a case regarding corporal punishment lawfully inflicted by police officers (in the Isle of Man) and held that it was a breach of Article 3 as it caused degrading and humiliating punishment.

There have been a number of cases relating to corporal punishments carried out in schools (in 'loco parentis') and these have generally held to be lawful where the punishments were not 'improper, inappropriate and disproportionate'. However, it is now unlawful for local authority, special and grant-maintained schools to use any form of corporal punishment and courts in the UK have convicted teachers of assault, despite being severely provoked by their charges.

Furthermore, the European Court has held that there is positive duty on the State to take appropriate measures to protect children from abuse and serious breaches of their personal integrity. Therefore, the work of Child Protection officers is recognised as a necessary function to uphold the rights of children and vulnerable individuals.

10.5. Glossary of human rights terms (alphabetical order)

ACPO	Association of Chief Police Officers of England, Wales and Northern Ireland
ASBO	Anti-social Behaviour Order
Accountability/Independent public remedy	Liability - to be answerable for one's conduct
Audit	Examination of records or accounts to check accuracy
CPIA	Criminal Procedure and Investigations Act 1996
Compatibility	Capable of efficient integration with each other
Compliance	In accordance with the law and principles of ECHR
Derogation	Deviation from a standard or expectation
ECHR	European Convention on Human Rights
EctHR	European Court of Human Rights
Entrapment	A legal term of art which describes circumstances where a person has been induced to commit an offence which he or she would not have committed but for the inducement
Equality of arms	All parties to a court case must have the same access to information and evidence
HRA	Human Rights Act 1998
Legality	In compliance with the law - lawful
Legitimate aims	Where infringements of citizen's rights occur, public authorities must be able to justify them through a 'legitimate aim' such as prevention of disorder or crime
Living instrument	Courts will interpret the law to reflect current standards in society, it therefore reflects current thinking and the modern culture in society
Margin of appreciation	Slight differences in the law to reflect the differences in culture in the different signatory countries to ECHR
Necessity	An essential requirement
PACE	Police and Criminal Evidence Act 1984
PEACE	PEACE method of interviewing - a mnemonic for: Preparation and planning; Engage and explain; Account/clarify/challenge; Closure; Evaluation
PPE	Personal protective equipment
Proportionality	There must be a reasonable relationship between the aim to be achieved and the means used
Relevance	Pertinence, relation to the matter in hand
Reservation	A keeping back or withholding
RIPA	Regulation of Investigatory Powers Act 2000

10.6. ECHR aide mémoire

European Convention on Human Rights Aide Mémoire

Use of Police Powers and decision-making for police officers and support staff

Do I have a lawful power?	Every action must have a legal basis.
Is what I am doing proportionate?	Is there a reasonable relationship between the aim to be achieved and the means used?
What is my objective?	What is the proposed action intended to achieve? Is it relevant and is it necessary?
Is there a less intrusive alternative?	Consider whether the objective can be achieved with less impact on the rights of the subject and any other person likely to be affected.
Do I need to act now?	Is the proposed action urgent or could it wait?
Is there a record of my reasoning?	Keep a record of the basis for your decisions whenever they affect someone's rights.

European Convention on Human Rights Articles and Protocols

Article 2	Right to life
Article 3	Prohibition of torture
Article 4	Prohibition of slavery
Article 5	Right to liberty and security
Article 6	Right to a fair trial
Article 7	No punishment without law
Article 8	Respect for private and family life
Article 9	Freedom of thought, conscience and religion
Article 10	Freedom of expression
Article 11	Freedom of assembly
Article 12	Freedom to marry
Article 14	Prohibition of discrimination

Articles 16,17,18
Political activity of aliens, abuse of rights, restriction on rights

First Protocol
Protection of property
Right to education
Right to free elections

Sixth Protocol
Abolition of the death penalty
Death penalty in time of war

PART FOUR

EVIDENCE

CHAPTER 11

INTERVIEWS AND MEDICAL EXAMINATIONS - CONSENT OF VICTIMS

11.1. Medical examinations

'Working Together Under the Children Act 1989' Appendix 2 Paragraph 1.4

If a child is of sufficient understanding, medical treatment may only be given with her or his consent (except in a medical emergency). It is for the doctor to decide whether the child is capable of giving consent if the child is under 16 years. Children of 16 years and over can give their own consent.

If the child is not of sufficient understanding, the consent of the parent, including a person with parental responsibility, is required. This would include the local authority if the child is subject to a care order.

Children who are capable of giving consent cannot be medically examined or assessed without their consent when subject to a child assessment, emergency protection, or an interim care or supervision order. In addition, children cannot be examined, assessed or treated in accordance with a full supervision order without their consent.

If there is a dispute in other circumstances in which a child refuses to consent, the matter may be put before a court to resolve.

11.2. Interviews

'Memorandum of Good Practice on Video Recorded Interviews with Child Witnesses for Criminal Proceedings' Paragraphs 2.29 and 2.30

If a child is mature enough to understand the concept, she or he should be given an explanation of the purpose of the video recording so that the child is fully informed – to a level appropriate to her or his age and understanding – and freely consents to the interview session and the video recording.

It should be explained that the video recording may be shown to the court instead of the child giving her or his account directly. The child should be advised that, whether a video recording is made or not, she or he may be required to attend court to answer questions directly.

Written consent to be video recorded is not necessary but it is unlikely to be practicable or desirable to video record an interview with a reluctant or distressed child.

When the child is too young to understand fully, the investigative team should listen to the views of the parent or carer. However, they should guard against the possibility of anyone who may be implicated in abuse of the child exerting any pressure on the child not to give her or his account.

Notes to 11.1. and 11.2.

In addition to this, guidelines issued by most local authorities require that consent, either to interview or to enable a medical examination to take place, is forthcoming from at least one person with **'parental responsibility'** – unless some form of court order to the contrary exists.

The form that this consent should take is often prescribed in such guidelines. There may also be some indication in these guidelines of the degree to which the requirement for such consent can be waived in the case of older children (who may be **'of sufficient understanding'**).

Taking a child into police protection does NOT provide the police with parental responsibility for the purposes of giving consent to an interview or to conduct a medical examination. In cases in which the consent of a person with parental responsibility for a child in police protection is not forthcoming, police will need to consider making an application for an emergency protection order with a condition authorising a medical examination or an interview under Section 44(6)(b) of the Children Act 1989 (Emergency Protection Orders - see 2.2).

See also Chapter 10 on Article 8, Respect for Private and Family Life (10.4d).

CHAPTER 12

TAKING SAMPLES FROM THOSE SUSPECTED OF HAVING COMMITTED OFFENCES

12.1. Intimate samples

> Section 65 Police and Criminal Evidence Act 1984 (as amended by the Criminal Justice and Public Order Act 1994)
>
> **'Intimate sample'** means a sample of blood, semen or any other tissue fluid, urine or pubic hair, a dental impression or a swab taken from a person's body orifice – other than the mouth

Section 62 Police and Criminal Evidence Act 1984 (as amended by the Criminal Justice and Public Order Act 1994)

Ss (1)
An intimate sample may be taken from a person in **'police detention'** only:

(a) if a police officer of at least the rank of Superintendent authorises it to be taken; and

(b) if the **'appropriate consent'** is given.

Ss (1A)
An intimate sample may be taken from a person who is not in police detention but from whom – in the course of an investigation of an offence – two or more non-intimate samples suitable for the same means of analysis have been taken which have proved insufficient:

(a) if a police officer of at least the rank of Superintendent authorises it to be taken; and

(b) if the appropriate consent is given.

Ss (2)
An officer may only give an authorisation under Sub-section (1) or (1A) above if she or he has reasonable grounds:

(a) for suspecting the person from whom the sample is to be taken to be involved in a **'recordable offence'**; and

(b) for believing that the sample will tend to confirm or disprove her or his involvement.

Ss (3)
An officer may give an authorisation under Sub-sections (1) or (1A) either orally or in writing, but, if she or he gives it orally, she or he shall confirm it in writing as soon as is practicable.

Ss (4)
The appropriate consent must be given in writing.

Ss (5)
When:

(a) an authorisation has been given; and

(b) it is proposed that an intimate sample shall be taken in pursuance of the authorisation;

an officer shall inform the person from whom the sample is to be taken –

i. of the giving of the authorisation, and
ii. of the grounds for giving it.

Ss (6)
The duty imposed by Sub-section (5)(ii) above includes a duty to state the nature of the offence in which it is suspected that the person from whom the sample is to be taken has been involved.

Ss (7)
If an intimate sample is to be taken from a person:

(a) the authorisation by virtue of which it was taken;

(b) the grounds for giving the authorisation; and

(c) the fact that the appropriate consent was given;

shall be recorded as soon as is practicable after the sample is taken.

Ss (7A)

If an intimate sample is taken from a person at a police station:

(a) an officer shall inform the person – before the sample is taken – that it may be the subject of a **'speculative search'**; and

(b) the fact that the person has been informed of this possibility shall be recorded as soon as practicable after the sample has been taken.

Ss (8)

If an intimate sample is taken from a person detained at a police station, the matters required to be recorded by Sub-sections (7) and (7A) above shall be recorded in the person's custody record.

Ss (9)

An intimate sample – other than a sample of urine or a dental impression – may only be taken from a person by a registered medical practitioner – and a dental impression may only be taken by a registered dentist.

Ss (10)

If the appropriate consent to the taking of an intimate sample from a person is refused without good cause, in any proceedings against that person for an offence:

(a) the court, in determining -
   i. whether to grant an application for dismissal made during the course of proceedings intended to transfer the case for trial under Section 6 Magistrates' Court Act 1980, or
   ii. whether there is a case to answer; and

(aa) a judge in deciding whether to grant an application made by the accused under –
   i. Section 6 Criminal Justice Act 1987 (application for dismissal of a charge of serious fraud in respect of which notice of transfer has been given under Section 4 of that Act), or
   ii. Paragraph 5 of Schedule 6 to the Criminal Justice Act 1991 (application for dismissal of a charge of a violent or sexual offence involving a child in respect of which notice has been given under Section 53 of that Act); and

(b) the court or jury, in determining whether that person is guilty of the offence charged;

may draw such inferences from the refusal as appear proper.

Notes

'Police detention'. A person is in police detention for the purposes of the Police and Criminal Act if:

(a) she or he has been taken to a police station after being arrested for an offence; or

(b) she or he is arrested at a police station after attending voluntarily at the station or accompanying a constable to it;

and is detained there or is detained elsewhere in the charge of a constable – except that a person who is at a court after being charged is not in police detention for these purposes (Section 118(2) Police and Criminal Evidence Act 1984).

'Appropriate consent' means:

(a) in relation to a person who has attained the age of 17 years, the consent of that person;

(b) in relation to a person who has not attained that age but has attained the age of 14 years, the consent of that person and her or his parent or guardian;

(c) in relation to a person who has not attained the age of 14 years, the consent of her or his parent or guardian

(Section 65 Police and Criminal Evidence Act 1984).

If anyone appears to be under the age of 17 years then she or he shall be treated as a juvenile in the absence of clear evidence to show she or he is older (Codes of Practice to the Police and Criminal Evidence Act 1984, Code D, Paragraph 1.4).

The consent of a suspected person who is suffering from a **'mental disorder'** or a mental handicap is only valid if given in the presence of an **'appropriate adult'** (Codes of Practice to the Police and Criminal Evidence Act 1984, Code D, Paragraph 1.11).

'Mental disorder' means 'mental illness, arrested or incomplete development of mind, psychopathic disorder and any other disorder or disability of mind' (Section 1(2) Mental Health Act 1983 as quoted in the Codes of Practice to the Police and Criminal Evidence Act 1984, Code D, Paragraph 1H).

If an officer has any suspicion, or is told in good faith – that a person of any age may be suffering from a mental disorder or is mentally handicapped – or may be mentally incapable of understanding the significance of questions put to her or him, or of her or his replies – then the person should be treated as a mentally disordered or mentally handicapped person.

If anyone appears to be under the age of 17 years then she or he shall be treated as a juvenile in the absence of clear evidence to show she or he is older (Codes of Practice to the Police and Criminal Evidence Act 1984, Code D, Paragraph 1.3).

The **'appropriate adult'** means, in the case of a person who is mentally disordered or mentally handicapped:

i. a relative, guardian or some other person responsible for her or his care or custody; or
ii. someone who has experience of dealing with mentally disordered or mentally handicapped persons – but is not a police officer or employed by the police – eg an approved social worker);
iii. failing either of the above, some other responsible adult aged 18 years or over who is not a police officer or employed by the police.

(The Codes of Practice to the Police and Criminal Evidence Act 1984, Code C Paragraph 1.7 and Code D, Paragraph 1.6.)

When clothing needs to be removed in circumstances likely to cause embarrassment to the person, no person of the opposite sex who is not a medical practitioner or nurse shall be present – unless in the case of a juvenile or a mentally disordered or mentally handicapped person, and that person specifically requests the presence of an appropriate adult of the opposite sex who is readily available – and no person shall be present whose presence is unnecessary. However, in the case of a juvenile this is subject to the overriding proviso that such a removal of clothing may take place in the absence of the appropriate adult only if the juvenile signifies, in the presence of the appropriate adult, that she or he prefers the search to be done in her or his absence and the appropriate adult agrees (Codes of Practice to the Police and Criminal Evidence Act 1984, Code D, Paragraph 5.12).

The **'appropriate adult'** means, in the case of a juvenile:

i. her or his parent or guardian (or the local authority if she or he is the subject of a care order);
ii. a social worker;
iii. failing either of the above, another responsible adult aged 18 years or over who is not a police officer or employed by the police;

(Codes of Practice to the Police and Criminal Evidence Act 1984, Code C Paragraph 1.7 and Code D, Paragraph 1.6).

'Recordable offences' refer to those offences for which convictions may be recorded in national police records. These are any offences which carry a sentence of imprisonment (irrespective of whether the individual is actually sent to prison) – and some non-imprisonable offences, specifically – loitering or soliciting for the purposes of prostitution (Section 1 Street Offences Act 1959), improper use of a public telecommunications system (Section 43 Telecommunications Act 1984), tampering with motor vehicles (Section 25 Road Traffic Act 1988), sending letters etc with intent to cause distress or anxiety (Section 1 Malicious Communications Act 1988), having an article with a blade or point in a public place (Section 139(1) Criminal Justice Act 1988) (in accordance with the Regulations made by the Home Secretary by virtue of The National Police Records (Recordable Offences) Regulations 1985).

'Speculative search' 'means that a check may be made against other samples – and information derived from other samples – contained in records- or held by or on behalf of the police – or held in connection with or as a result of an investigation of an offence' (Codes of Practice to the Police and Criminal Evidence Act1984, Code D, Paragraph 5D).

12.2. Non-intimate samples

> Section 65 Police and Criminal Evidence Act 1984 as amended by the Criminal Justice and Public Order Act 1994
>
> **'Non-intimate sample'** means:
>
> (a) a sample of hair other than pubic hair;
>
> (b) a sample taken from a nail or from under a nail:
>
> (c) a swab taken from any part of a person's body including the mouth but not any other body orifice;
>
> (d) saliva;
>
> (e) a footprint or a similar impression of any part of a person's body other than a part of her or his hand.

Section 63 Police and Criminal Evidence Act 1984 (as amended by the Criminal Justice and Public Order Act 1994)

Ss (1)

Except as provided by this Section, a non-intimate sample may not be taken from a person without the **'appropriate consent'**.

Ss (2)

Consent to the taking of a non-intimate sample must be given in writing.

Ss (3)

A non-intimate sample may be taken from a person without the appropriate consent if:

(a) she or he is in police detention or is being held in custody by the police on the authority of a court; and

(b) an officer of at least the rank of Superintendent authorises it to be taken without the appropriate consent.

Ss (3A)

A non-intimate sample may be taken from a person (whether or not she or he falls within Sub-section (3)(a) above) without the appropriate consent if:

(a) she or he has been charged with a **'recordable offence'**, or informed that she or he will be reported for such an offence;

(b) she or he either has not had a non-intimate sample taken from her or him in the course of the investigation of the offence by police – or she or he has had a non-intimate sample taken from her or him but either it was not suitable for the same means of analysis or, though suitable, it proved insufficient.

Ss (3B)

A non-intimate sample may be taken from a person without consent if she or he has been convicted of a recordable offence.

Ss (3C)

A non-intimate sample may also be taken from a person without the appropriate consent if she or he is a person to whom Section 2 Criminal Evidence (Amendment) Act 1997 applies (persons detained following acquittal on grounds of insanity or having been found unfit to plead).

Ss (4)

An officer may only give authorisation under Sub-section (3) above, if she or he has reasonable grounds:

(a) for suspecting the involvement of the person from whom the sample is to be taken in a recordable offence; and

(b) for believing that the sample will tend to confirm or disprove her or his involvement.

Ss (5)

An officer may give an authorisation under Sub-section (3) above either orally or in writing, but, if she or he gives it orally, she or he shall confirm it in writing as soon as is practicable.

Ss (6)

When:

(a) an authorisation has been given; and

(b) it is proposed that a non-intimate sample shall be taken in pursuance of the authorisation;

an officer shall inform the person from whom the sample is to be taken -

i. of the giving of the authorisation, and
ii. of the grounds for giving it.

Ss (7)
The duty imposed by Sub-section (6)(b)(ii) above includes a duty to state the nature of the offence in which it is suspected that the person from whom the sample is to be taken has been involved.

Ss (8)
If a non-intimate sample is taken from a person by virtue of Sub-section (3) (previous page):

(a) the authorisation by virtue of which it was taken; and

(b) the grounds for giving the authorisation;

shall be recorded as soon as is practicable after the sample is taken.

Ss (8A)
In a case in which a non-intimate sample is taken from a person without consent under Sub-sections (3A), (3B) or (3C):

(a) she or he will be told the reason, before the sample is taken; and

(b) the reason shall be recorded as soon as is practicable after the sample is taken.

Ss (8B)
If a non-intimate sample is taken from a person at a police station, whether with or without the appropriate consent:

(a) before the sample is taken, an officer shall inform her or him that it may be the subject of a **'speculative search'**; and

(b) the fact that the person has been informed of this possibility shall be recorded as soon as practicable after the sample has been taken.

Ss (9)
If a non-intimate sample is taken from a person detained at a police station, the matters required to be recorded by Sub-sections (8), 8(A) or 8(B) above shall be recorded on the person's custody record.

Ss (9B)
Sub-section (3B) shall not apply to any person convicted before 10.4.95 unless she or he is a person to whom Section 1 Criminal Evidence (Amendment) Act 1997 applies (persons imprisoned or detained by virtue of a pre-existing conviction for a sexual offence etc).

Notes

'Appropriate consent', **'recordable offence'** and **'speculative search'** are all as defined in Intimate Samples (see 12.1).

If a non-intimate sample is to be taken by the police from a person without consent under Sub-sections (3), (3A) and (3B) then, **'reasonable force'** may be used (Section 117 Police and Criminal Evidence Act1984).

See also Chapter 10 on Article 8, Respect for Private and Family Life (10.4d).

CHAPTER 13

VIDEO INTERVIEWING CHILD WITNESSES

Sections 52 – 55 Criminal Justice Act 1991

The above Sections of the Criminal Justice Act 1991 and the accompanying 'Memorandum of Good Practice' came into effect on 1.10.92.

Neither this part of the Criminal Justice Act nor the 'Memorandum of Good Practice' are mandatory. However, the extent to which other interviewing methods are likely to prove acceptable to the courts remains an open question.

The underlying purpose of these Sections is to reduce the amount of stress endured by children giving evidence in criminal cases.

The 'Memorandum of Good Practice' clearly states that these interviews should only be conducted by those with the training experience and aptitude for talking to children and who are properly conversant with the Memorandum.

The Criminal Justice Act and the 'Memorandum of Good Practice' are both likely to be superseded in 2002 or 2003 when the Youth Justice and Criminal Evidence Act 1999 comes into force (implementation date not yet published).This Act will significantly expand the entitlement to video recorded witness testimony and will be accompanied by a document that will replace the 'Memorandum of Good Practice'.

In its consultation draft form, this new document is entitled 'Achieving Best Evidence in Criminal Proceedings: Guidance for Vulnerable or Intimidated Witnesses, Including Children' and can currently be perused on the Internet at http://www.homeoffice.gov.uk/cpg/vulncont.htm

13.1. Memorandum of Good Practice

Following an introduction, the 'Memorandum of Good Practice' is divided into four Sections. The relevant points in each Section are set as follows.

PART 1

Scope

The Criminal Justice Act 1991 provides for the use of video tapes from interviews with alleged victims /witnesses in the following circumstances:

i. in respect of **'violent offences'** in which the alleged victim/witness is under 14 years of age at the time that the video is made (under 15 years at the time of the trial);

ii. in respect of **'sexual offences'** in which the alleged victim/witness is under 17 years of age at the time that the video is made (under 18 years at the time of the trial).

It is intended that video tapes made in accordance with the Memorandum of Good Practice be used as evidence-in-chief in trials at the Crown or youth court. Except in certain exceptional circumstances, the child will still need to go to court to be cross examined (although this may take place on a live video-link system).

The video tapes cannot be used in a trial at a magistrates' court. Section 53 of the Criminal Justice Act 1991 allows the Crown Prosecution Service by the service of a 'notice of transfer' to effectively by-pass committal proceedings in cases that it is intended the Crown court should hear.

'Violent offences' are defined as ANY offence involving an assault on, injury to, or the threat of injury to a person – or any offence contrary to Section 1 Children and Young Persons Act 1933 (cruelty etc). **'Sexual offences'** are defined as any offence contrary to the Sexual Offences Act 1956; the Indecency with Children Act 1960; the Sexual Offences Act 1967; Section 54Criminal Law Act 1977 or the Protection of Children Act 1978.

Pre-interview contact

The Memorandum of Good Practice suggests that any early discussions with the child should, so far as is possible, adhere to the following basic principles:

a. listen to the child, rather than directly question her or him;
b. never stop a child who is freely recalling significant events;
c. make a note of the discussion, taking care to record the timing, setting and personnel present as well as what was said; and
d. record all subsequent events up to the time of the substantive interview;

(Paragraph 1.8 Memorandum of Good Practice).

Ideal equipment

The Memorandum of Good Practice recommends use of equipment of the type that is often available at interview suites especially built for the purpose of conducting investigative interviews with children and young people. This is high quality recording equipment containing such features as wall microphones and a picture-in-picture facility. In the absence of this ideal, the Memorandum allows the use of any equipment able to deliver good sound and vision quality (Paragraphs 1.17 – 1.21 Memorandum of Good Practice).

PART 2

This part of the Memorandum deals with the planning of the interview including the pre-interview assessment of the child's competence as a potential witness. The Memorandum views this planning as crucial and states that a plan of the interview – including clearly defined objectives – should always be drawn up (Paragraph 2.1 Memorandum of Good Practice).

At the planning stage, information should be gathered in respect of the following areas of the child's development:

a. cognitive (reasoning) ability (including the child's attention span and concept of time);
b. language use;
c. emotional development (including the child's present state of mind);
d. nature and quality of her or his social relationships;
e. sexual/psycho sexual development; and
f. physical development.

A consideration of all these areas should include a great deal of thought to the child's gender and background and any disabilities she or he may suffer from (Paragraphs 2.3 to 2.10, Memorandum of Good Practice).

The objectives and the information gathered in respect of the child should be used to determine:

a. whether or not an interview takes place;
b. who conducts any interview; and
c. the structure, style, duration and pace of any such interview.

Evidence of this planning process may be called for in court (Paragraph 2.25 Memorandum of Good Practice) and will thus probably be required by the Crown Prosecution Service beforehand.

PART 3

This part of the Memorandum of Good Practice recommends a structure in which the interview should take place and notes the legal constraints involved in conducting these interviews. Specifically, the structure of the interview refers to the four-phased approach of:

1. rapport;
2. free narrative;
3. questioning; sub-divided into –
   i. open questions,
   ii. specific non-leading questions,
   iii. closed questions,
   iv. leading questions;
4. end phase.

The legal constraints refer to:

a. leading questions;
b. hearsay evidence; and
c. statements of the character of the accused person.

In addition, the Memorandum places constraints upon the use of 'genitalled dolls' (Appendix 1) and a 'facilitative style of questioning' (Appendix 2).

Beyond this, the Memorandum does not deal with specific interview techniques that should be used in communicating with children. At this level non-leading trigger techniques (means of encouraging the child to talk about the circumstances relating to the allegation) and ways of managing the child's potential blocking mechanisms (reasons why the child may not wish to talk to the interviewer) need to be considered.

The Memorandum also states that the legal framework set out in Part 3 should not be departed from unless the investigating team has consulted its senior managers (Paragraph 3.1 Memorandum of Good Practice).

PART 4

This part of the Memorandum deals with the security of the tapes after the interview. In essence, the tapes are to be stored securely and copying of and access to them should be kept to a minimum.

A log book is to be kept in respect of these tapes and this should be the subject of periodic inspection by management.

The following section on Planning the Interview provides a summary of the information required to plan an interview in accordance with the Memorandum of Good Practice and gives a sample of one possible way in which this information might be used in the planning process.

13.2. Planning the interview

1. Gather information relating to the child

This information should be respect of the child's development specifically concerning –

- cognitive,
- linguistic,
- social,
- emotional,
- sexual, and
- physical issues;

and also the child's -

- concept of time,
- ideas about trust,
- present state of mind,
- gender,
- cultural background,
- disabilities.

2. Consider communication issues

Consider any blocks that might impede the child from communicating with the interviewers and think about any possible ways for dealing with them.

3. Set objectives for the interview

Interview objectives should be on the basis of –

- the initial referral, and
- any other information obtained during preliminary checks.

4. Decide whether to interview

This decision will be based on all the information gained from the above three stages. If you are going to conduct an interview, then consider –

- style (facilitative or investigative),
- structure (if investigative, the four phases of the Memorandum of Good Practice or other appropriate structure),
- duration (according to the Memorandum of Good Practice this should generally be no more than about an hour), and
- pace of the interview (the child's pace as suggested by the information gathered at stage **1.** above) including breaks in the interview.

5. Decide upon your interviewers

This decision will be in the light of all the above information. Decide who is to take the lead and pre-arrange signals between interviewers.

6. Plan the interview

Make use of all the information you have about the child and take account of your objectives. While doing this, bear in mind the legal constraints (leading questions/techniques, previous statements made by the child, statements as to the character of the accused person and the use of 'genitalled dolls' and a 'facilitative style of questioning'). If you find it appropriate and helpful use the format provided in the sample below.

7. Written record

Make a written record of the entire planning process – it may well be called for in court.

Sample

Format/planning issues for planning an interview in accordance with the Memorandum of Good Practice

1 Check equipment.

2 Turn on tapes, give personal introductions, state day, date, time and place.

3 Rapport phase

- Tell the child why she or he is there without referring to the alleged offence. *(How are you going to do this?)*
- Do or talk about something in order to build rapport – again without referring to the alleged offence. *(What are you going to do/talk about?)*
- Tell the child that if you ask her or him any questions later on it is all right for them to say that they don't know or don't understand.
- Tell the child that if she or he decides to say anything to you later on it is important that they tell you everything that they can remember without leaving anything out or making anything up.

4 Free narrative phase

Try to 'trigger' a free narrative account from the child. If you are successful, support this by the use of only minimal prompts. *(How will you try to 'trigger' a free narrative account? Ideally have at least two or three options.)*

5 Questions phase

Ask questions necessary to clarify what was said during the free narrative account. This would include asking any questions necessary to prove any offences disclosed. *(It might help here if you could check Annex D of the Memorandum of Good Practice and discuss the necessary contextual questions with your co-interviewer while you are planning the interview.)*

Any questions should, as far as possible, follow the following sequence:

- open questions;
- specific non-leading questions;
- closed questions.

Leading questions should only be used if absolutely necessary. If an evidentially valid response is made to such a question then the interviewer should return to one of the more open stages of the interview in a bid to validate that response.*

* For example, should an officer ask a child, 'Has anyone else ever done anything like this to you?' and the child responds, 'Yes, uncle X did things to me,' the officer must immediately revert to an open question such as, 'Tell me about this…'. The officer then has a basis to refute any assumption that further detail provided by the child is solely a response to suggestion.

6 Ending phase

- Consider summarising using the child's own words if this appears to be necessary. *(If you decide to do this, how will you do it? Who will actually summarise, the lead or the support interviewer? Should the support interviewer write down what the child says to facilitate such a summary?)*
- Consider returning to what you did to settle the child during the rapport phase.
- Thank the child and give the child (or appropriate adult) a contact number where you and your co-interviewer may be contacted.
- State the time and switch off the tape.
- The practice guidance set out in the document entitled 'Provision of Therapy for Child Witnesses Prior to a Criminal Trial (published jointly by the Home Office, Crown Prosecution Service and Department of Health in 2001) should be adhered to in the event of a child witness requiring therapy following an interview and prior to giving evidence at a trial.

CHAPTER 14

PREPARING CHILD WITNESSES TO GIVE EVIDENCE IN COURT

14.1. The effects of the legal process upon the child witness

Over recent years there has been much concern as to the effects of the legal process upon the child witness. Indeed, it might be said that this was at least one of the reasons why the 'Memorandum of Good Practice on Video Recorded Interviews with Child Witnesses for Criminal Proceedings' (HMSO 1992) was devised.

Unfortunately very little research has been conducted in this respect (Flin *et al*, 1989). Such empirical evidence as does exist tends to support the commonly held notion that children find their involvement in legal proceedings to be stressful (for example, Goodman and Jones 1988).

One of the possible sources of such stress may lie in children's lack of knowledge of court proceedings. Until the late 1980s most of the studies designed to investigate children's knowledge of legal proceedings were conducted outside the United Kingdom, in the United States and Australia.

In 1989, however, Flin, Stevenson and Davies reported the findings of a study they had conducted in Scotland in respect of six, eight and 10-year-old children. These findings were broadly consistent with studies previously conducted in other countries.

The findings of Flin *et al* suggest that there are some important deficits and misconceptions in a child's knowledge of court proceedings. These relate to the roles of the participants in the proceedings and to the process itself. This was especially true of the six and eight-year-old age groups in their sample.

For example, while many children had some conception of 'policeman', 'rule', 'promise' and 'truth', they did not understand the terms 'going to court', 'evidence', 'jury', 'lawyer', 'prosecute', 'trial' and 'witness'. Some of the children had misconceptions of some legal terms, for example one common misapprehension was that a person who was to be prosecuted would be 'hung', 'killed' or 'jailed'.

When asked about their feelings about going to court, some of the children also had some gaps in their knowledge and held misconceptions such as the notion that mainly 'bad people' went to court.

In addition to this and, perhaps, most worrying, was the reasons that some of the children gave for feeling nervous about going to court. These were fears of not being believed and often, in consequence, a fear of being sent to prison.

14.2. The child witness pack

Concerns such as these outlined above were responsible for the development of the Child Witness Pack. The pack was developed by the Home Office, the Lord Chancellor's Department, the Crown Prosecution Service, the Department of Health, ChildLine, The Children's Society, the Children's legal centre, the NSPCC and the National Children's Bureau. It was co-ordinated by Joyce Polnikoff and Anne Markowycz.

The pack may be used to prepare any child witness for her or his appearance at a criminal court – irrespective of the nature of the offences with which the defendant is charged – although the use of a live video-link remains restricted to those offences specified by the Criminal Justice Act 1991 (as shown in the previous chapter on Video Interviewing Child Witnesses, Part 1 of the Memorandum of Good Practice - see 13.1).

The pack itself consists of three booklets:

Let's get ready for Court
for 'younger' children (five to nine-year-olds).

Tell me more about Court
'for 'older' children (10 to 15-year-olds).

Your Child is a Witness
for parents/carers of child witnesses.

The material in the booklets for child witnesses is intended to be used interactively between the child and an **'independent adult'**.

For a person to be independent she or he should 'not have been involved in the detailed preparation of the case'.

The independent adult should 'ideally':

- have an awareness of the needs of abused children;
- be knowledgeable about the criminal justice system;
- have the confidence of the police and Crown Prosecution Service and have the ability to work with other agencies;
- be familiar with the basic rules of evidence and the dangers of inadvertently contaminating or otherwise discrediting the child's evidence;
- have a working knowledge of the relevant sections of the Memorandum of Good Practice on Video Recorded Interviews with Child Witnesses for Criminal Proceedings.

Copies of the 'Child Witness Pack' may be obtained from the NSPCC.

14.3. Child witness update

At the time of going to press, the only Sections in the Youth Justice and Criminal Evidence Act 1999 that have been implemented are those:

- prohibiting cross-examination by a defendant in person (Sections 34 - 40);
- limiting the extent to which the sexual history of a complainant in a sexual assault case can be introduced in court (Sections 41 and 42).

It is anticipated that the giving of evidence by child and other vulnerable witnesses will be further enhanced when the Act is more fully implemented.

In addition to this, when the Youth Justice and Criminal Evidence Act is implemented, the document that is to replace the *Memorandum of Good Practice on Video Recorded Interviews with Child Witnesses for Criminal Proceedings* will probably contain some national standards for the preparation of young witnesses attending court.

In draft form, this document is entitled, *Achieving Best Evidence in Criminal Proceedings: Guidance for Vulnerable or Intimidated Witnesses, Including Children,* and can currently be perused on the Home Office Website at:
http://www.homeoffice.gov.uk/cpg/vulncont.htm

CHAPTER 15

COMPELLABILITY OF SPOUSE WITNESSES

Section 80 Police and Criminal Evidence Act 1984

Ss (1)

In any proceedings, the wife or husband of the accused shall be competent to give evidence:

(a) subject to Sub-section (4) below, for the prosecution; and

(b) on behalf of the accused, or any person jointly charged with the accused.

Ss (2)

In any proceedings the wife or husband of the accused shall, subject to Sub-section (4), be compellable to give evidence on behalf of the accused.

Ss (3)

In any proceedings the wife or husband of the accused shall, subject to Sub-section (4), be compellable to give evidence for the prosecution or on behalf of any person jointly charged with the accused if, and only if:

(a) the offence charged involves an assault on, or injury or a threat of injury to the wife or husband of the accused or a person who is at the material time under the age of 16 years; or

(b) the offence charged is a sexual offence alleged to have been committed in respect of a person who was at the material time under that age; or

(c) the offence charged consists of attempting or conspiring to commit or of aiding, abetting, counselling, procuring or inciting the commission of an offence falling within Paragraph (a) or (b) of this Sub-section.

Ss (4)

If a husband and wife are jointly charged with an offence, neither spouse shall at the trial be competent or compellable by virtue of Sub-section (1)(a), (2) or (3) above to give evidence in respect of that offence unless that spouse is not, or is no longer, liable to be convicted of that offence at the trial as a result of pleading guilty, or for any other reason.

Ss (5)

In any proceedings, a person who has been but is no longer married to the accused shall be competent and compellable to give evidence as if that person and the accused had never been married.

Ss (6)

If in any proceedings, the age of any person at any time is material for the purpose of Sub-section (3) above. Her or his age at the material time shall for the purposes of that provision be deemed to be or to have been that which appears to the court to be or to have been her or his age at that time.

Ss (7)

In Sub-section (3)(b) above **'sexual offence'** means an offence under the Sexual Offences Act 1956; the Indecency with Children Act 1960; the Sexual Offences Act 1967; Section 54 Criminal Law Act 1977 or the Protection of Children Act 1978.

Ss (8)

The failure of the wife or husband of the accused to give evidence shall not be made the subject of any comment by the prosecution.

Note

A bigamous spouse is competent as, generally, is the wife of a second polygamous marriage (*R v Khan* 84 Cr App R 44 and *R v Yacoob* 72 Cr App R 313).

References

Draycott A T and Carr A P (eds) *Stone's Justices' Manual*, 113th Edition, London, Butterworths.

English J and Card R (1994) *Butterworths Police Law*, London, Butterworths.

Flin R H, Stevenson Y and Davies G M (1989) 'Children's Knowledge of Court Proceedings' *British Journal of Psychology*, 80, pp 285-297.

Goodman G S and Jones D P (1988) 'The Emotional Effects of Criminal Court Testimony on Child Sexual Assault Victims; a Preliminary Report' in Davies G and Drinkwater J (eds) *The Child Witness; Do the Courts Abuse Children?* Leicester, The British Psychological Society.

Lyon C and De Cruz P (1993) *Child Abuse*, Bristol, Jordan Publishing.

Murphy P (ed) (1998) *Blackstone's Criminal Practice*, 8th Edition, London, Blackstone Press.

Richardson P J (ed) (1998) *Archbold: Criminal Pleading, Evidence and Practice*, London, Sweet and Maxwell.

Further Reading on Human Rights

Beckley A (2000) *Human Rights: The Pocket Guide for Police Officers and Support Staff.* The New Police Bookshop, Surrey.
ISBN 1 903639 00 X Price £7:50

Beckley A (2000) *Human Rights: The Guide for Police Officers and Support Staff.* The New Police Bookshop, Surrey.
ISBN 1 903639 01 8 Price £12:50

Neyroud P & Beckley A (2000) *Policing Ethics & Human Rights,* Willan Publishing: Cullompton, Devon, UK.
ISBN: 1-903240-15-8 Price: £17.99

Starmer K (1999) *European Human Rights Law:* Legal Action Group, London.
ISBN 0 905099 77 X

Wadham J and Mountfield H (1999) *Guide to the Human Rights Act 1998* Blackstone Press, London. ISBN 1 85431 837 3 Price: £19.95

Index

A

B

C

The Child Protection Investigator's Companion is published by the New Police Bookshop (Surrey)

ISBN ISBN 1 903639 04 2 £13.50